Published in 2021 by The School of Life
First published in the USA in 2022
70 Marchmont Street, London WC1N 1AB

Designed by Marcia Mihotich
Typeset by Kerrypress
Printed in Latvia by Livonia

A proportion of this book has appeared online at
www.theschooloflife.com/thebookoflife

The School of Life is a resource for helping us understand
ourselves, for improving our relationships, our careers
and our social lives – as well as for helping us find calm
and get more out of our leisure hours. We do this through
creating films, workshops, books, apps and gifts.

www.theschooloflife.com

ISBN 978-1-912891-54-2

10 9 8 7 6 5 4 3 2 1

The
Good Enough
Parent

How to raise contented, interesting and resilient children

The School of Life

CONTENTS

Introduction

For most of history, the reasons why people had children had very little to do with children themselves. They had them because they needed extra manpower on the farm, or because they wanted someone to look after them in old age; because they were afraid of the judgement of society, because God ordered them to give birth, or because they were trying to ensure the continuity of the family business or the nation. The child itself, with its unique nature and needs, with its particular aspirations for fulfilment, was typically the last thing on anyone's mind. When it arrived, it was frequently treated little better than an animal; it was highly likely to die young and largely ignored until it had proved that it wouldn't – and it was forced to obey and listen rather than explore and question. It may have existed, but it was not remotely at the centre of existence.

The modern world has shifted this attitude entirely. We now live in a much more child-centric universe, and are deeply concerned with the welfare and development of our children on their own terms. Our goal is no longer to produce new humans in order to satisfy our needs; it is to put them on the Earth so that they may flourish. We are interested in their inner growth and authentic possibilities. As parents have been repeating for two generations at least, we only want them to be happy.

And yet, strangely, whatever the theoretical strength of our commitment to childcare, we haven't shown limitless imagination or thoroughness in our actions and methods. Our capacities lag behind our aspirations. We have been slow to shake off a naïve trust in instinct, clinging to an intuitive way of going about things, and we can be suspicious of any overly direct process of education. There remains for many of us something offensive about the notion of having to seek instruction in how to make conversation with a 5-year-old or how to cope with a melancholic adolescent. We assume that we will just know. We suppose that being a decent parent is something we feel our way towards, not something we could train for. This book disagrees.

The stakes could not be higher. Once viewed as a kind of long dream that meant nothing and could be forgotten about as soon as it was over, childhood is now conceived of as a momentously consequential period in which the entire emotional disposition of a person will be formed and their chances of a mentally healthy life determined. It is the curse of *Homo sapiens* to have been lumbered with an exceptionally long and susceptible period of maturation. A foal can stand up thirty minutes after its birth, a golden eaglet grows up in twelve weeks, a chimpanzee is an adult in nine years, yet it can be twenty years or more until a human can make its own bed or face life unaided. This exposes our species far more than is usual in the animal kingdom to the quirks and vagaries of parents. It probably wouldn't matter overly if a baby turtle's mother was emotionally detached or if a golden eagle's dad had a propensity to humiliate. But our species takes parental failings much more to heart. An unfortunate time between the ages of 1 and 9 has the power to unbalance a whole life; a depressive parent can permanently sap a child's energy to succeed.

This sensitivity explains the dread that accompanies many modern efforts at parenting. Parents are only too aware, as their 12th-century predecessors were not, that their choices at the dinner table or at bedtime can either lay down the foundations for sanity and hope or doom a child for the next eight decades. In the circumstances, it would be understandable if some of us were to seek out systematic instruction. The puzzle is how we could be expected to handle child-rearing without it, any more than we could understand the orbital path of Jupiter or the nature of the Martian atmosphere without taking time for some lessons.

Before we begin such instruction, we should dare to consider a nagging question: how many of us should actually be having children? The topic feels taboo. The assumption of modern societies is that every 'normal' person should seek to have children, and that no effort should be spared in enabling them to do so.

Yet wisdom may point us in a different direction. Many of us do not necessarily want to have children; we just feel an enormous pressure to produce them anyway. After a few years together, a young couple will face a barrage of questions as to when a baby will be on the way, and can expect to be judged harshly if they have no interest in delivering one.

Yet a society that properly loved children would know that the greatest factor contributing to children's welfare is the removal of the idea that everyone should automatically have them. A good society would give equal prestige to child-free and childful states. We best honour children, both the born and the unborn, by accepting that parenting should never be the automatic choice, just as the wisest way to ensure that people will have happy marriages is to destigmatise singlehood.

If we haven't travelled, if we don't yet know what we want, if we have a hard time staying with anyone for a while or remaining friendly with them when we part, if we like to be admired a lot, if our real passions lie at the office, if the purpose of our life is to be famous, if we don't especially like to listen, if we have trouble being calm, if we have been very badly scrambled by our own parents, then we might consider whether – in fairness to everyone involved – this is really for us. Some of the best people in existence do not make ideal parents; the truly great ones know this about themselves and act bravely on the knowledge.

In a better arranged world, a sizeable share of the population, perhaps a majority, would remain child-free. They would find life without offspring both challenging and rewarding enough. When they occasionally felt a desire for a child, they would be afforded plenty of opportunities to spend time with one for a while. Just as national museums have prevented most of us from needing to own masterpieces personally, so too might we spend an afternoon with a small treasure owned by someone else – mitigating any pressure or inclination to go and get one of our own.

Those who really wanted to have children might be considered in the same way as were, in the 9th century, the dedicated minority who left behind the ordinary comforts of existence in order to become nuns or priests. One would admire their devotion while privately shuddering at the price it had exacted.

In a painting by the Swiss artist Ferdinand Hodler, a young child sits on their mother's knee. The woman is carefully spooning some liquid, probably milk, from a cup. All those who have been in a similar position will instinctively know what a child that age might weigh, how cosy they would be to hold, how soft their hair would feel, how protectively one's hand would circle their chest and how touching would be their fascination with something as simple as a spoon. But the parent would know a few other things besides: how

Ferdinand Hodler, *Mother and Child*, 1888

rare these moments of peace generally are, how long it took to get the child dressed, how angry they were about having to put on boots, how quickly they will need another change, how loudly they can scream, how little recognition one is ever given for one's labours and how exhausted (and close to despair) one generally feels by bedtime.

The world is never unhappy because of children who have not yet been born; it is grief-stricken by children who have been placed on the planet without anyone to love or protect them adequately. We can cope with fewer children; what we need above all else are parents sufficiently dedicated to the tasks of love. This book is for them.

1. Lessons in Emotional Maturity

The most basic and never-to-be-forgotten fact about any infant is that it is born into a state of radical immaturity. It cannot understand its condition; it doesn't know how to communicate; it has no way of empathising; it can't help but be muddled about its own needs. Over many long years, it must be guided into developing into that most prized but elusive of beings: an emotionally mature adult.

The distinction between adult and infant is, confusingly, never assured by age alone. It cannot be determined simply by looking at someone's face and body, let alone their outward status or profession. There are nonagenarians who, in emotional aspects, are still mired in toddlerhood, and 9-year-olds who rival many so-called grown-ups in their responses to life's vicissitudes.

The curriculum of emotional maturity, of the journey between infancy and adulthood, encapsulates some of the following transitions:

- An infant believes, touchingly and unavoidably, that it is the centre of the universe. An adult has had to learn, through considerable sorrow and inconvenience, that other humans appear to exist as well.

- An infant insists vociferously on its wants. In its rages it is as categorical as a furious emperor. An adult has had to come to terms with the idea of compromise. It has learnt to be a diplomat. It has come to know that, oddly, there may be other points of view.

- An infant believes that others around it will be able to understand its wants and intentions without it needing to speak, that being loved means being magically understood, and falls into vicious sulks with those who do not correctly intuit its intentions. An adult has learnt the tedious requirement to speak calmly and explain the contents of its own mind: it has learnt to teach the world about itself.

- An infant cannot understand the influence of its body on its moods. It cannot tell that its despair has to do with tiredness or its excitement with an excess of sugar. An adult has learnt to coexist with its own body; it knows that at certain bleak-seeming moments, rather than giving up on humanity and its own life, it may simply need to drink a glass of water or have an early night.

- An infant is a relentless idealiser: those who please it are wondrous creatures to whom it freely gives affection and tenderness. By the same measure, those who frustrate it risk being framed as demons and monsters who deserve to be bitten or destroyed. An adult realises that there is no such thing as a wholly good or bad person; it does not fall in love quite so regularly – or in hate.

- An infant imagines that an adult must know exactly what it is doing. After all, it's so big, it can kick a ball many metres into the air and drive a car. An adult knows how to tread a more nuanced path between trust and scepticism; it knows, in a benign way, that everyone is to some degree making it up as they go along.

- An infant is not aware of the pain or inconvenience it puts others to. It is blithely and beautifully self-absorbed. An adult has acquired a correct measure of the difficulties it causes others, especially those it loves; it can feel appropriate degrees of guilt; it can say sorry.

- An infant is wildly and erratically afraid: of being eaten by tigers, of being destroyed by teachers, of being swept away by the wind. Some of these are its own aggressions projected outwards. The adult has correctly repatriated its fears. It has a sound sense of where terror belongs.

- An infant is often either in tears or delighted. An infant is a creature of hope constantly buffeted by disappointment, and capable of being instantly thrown into rage or ecstasy. An adult has acquired a talent for poised melancholy leavened by wry humour.

- An adult doesn't mind noticing aspects of its character that aren't wholly mature. An adult knows that, at moments, it will revert to infancy. A child, especially an adolescent one, will insist with telling and implausible vehemence that it is fully done with childhood.

- An adult is someone who knows how to look after a child – chiefly because, somewhere in a fortunate past, someone else nurtured the child-like parts of them.

These lessons and many others like them belong to the process known as emotional education. Tediously, this cannot be imparted quickly. It may take at least five times as long as learning how to master a foreign language. Patience, therefore, has to be one of the central prerequisites of any parental instructor. The module on the unyielding nature of reality will, for example, have to be taught on a thousand occasions before it takes root: over Nounou's broken eye, a sudden stain on a favourite pair of trousers, the end of screen time, the miserableness of going to bed, the boringness of the long car ride, the death of Granny, the entirely unnecessary arrival of a sibling – and a thousand other tragedies, small and large, besides.

Unlike a curriculum for a language, the emotional curriculum lacks a well-defined timetable. There aren't clear sections like those on improper fractions or the use of the definitive article; one can't limit lessons to Thursday afternoons or Monday mornings. There will be days when five separate learning modules will have to be taught before breakfast is over, and with no warning of an upcoming challenge having been given. The child is at all times on the journey of striving to become a grown-up. Every waking minute the young brain is pushing on to become the more mature self it is destined to become. This doesn't mean that emotional maturity is what everyone will eventually accede to, no more than every oak tree will reach the forty metres of which it is biologically capable; it simply means that this is the direction an infant is oriented towards and will be striving for unless impediments are placed in its way.

It is worth emphasising that all elements of immaturity – egocentricity, boastfulness, idealisation and so on – belong to health at a given age. The child has to go through every stage of juvenility in order one day to settle into an authentically mature position.

Parents who succeed at teaching the emotional curriculum should not expect particular prizes or signs of gratitude. The reward, if and when it comes, will be more indirect but all the more sincere for that: an offspring who is inwardly alive, who can be kind to themselves and knows how to care for less mature, still struggling others – perhaps, most touchingly, their own offspring.

2. Lessons in Love

Strangely, and rather inconveniently, it seems no human being can really grow up entirely well balanced unless it has been loved very deeply by someone for a number of years in its early life. But we're still learning what parental love might actually involve. The word 'love' trips lightly off the tongue. Few parents – even the most disagreeable ones – would deny that they felt the emotion deeply, but that doesn't mean that loving behaviour is any easier to understand in theory or enact in reality.

What then might be some of the principles of parental love? The start of a list might look like this:

Attunement

A loving parent gets down to the child's level – at times literally, dropping to their height when addressing them – in order to see the world through their eyes.

They understand that a very young child cannot easily fit in with external demands and that, in the early days, they must be prioritised and placed at the centre of things, not in order to 'spoil' them, but in order to give them a chance to grow. They will need to have been doted on for long enough in order that, eventually, they can develop into generous, empathetic and self-contented adults. Loving parents instinctively understand that what 'attention-seeking' children need isn't punishment and a lecture about being difficult, but the right kind of attuned care that will coax them out of their frantic bids for love.

Vulnerability

Loving parents know the physical and psychological vulnerability of a young child and are ready to feel sorry for them rather than use their weakness as an occasion to avenge themselves for their own privations; sorry for how much they don't understand, for how hard it is for them to communicate, for how strange their tummies can feel or how angry they can become without any option for release other than a scream. The parent can allow them to be little for a long time, because they can see over the horizon to the eventual emergence of a capable adult.

Small things

Loving parents understand that their young offspring's lives revolve around details that are, by any adult measure, very minor. Toddlers will feel happy because they can dig their nails into some putty or have a chance to whack their spoon into some peas with energy or say 'bah' very loudly; and they will feel sad because their toy rabbit lost one of its buttons or a page in a favourite book now has a tear in it. These parents will know that, at moments, the whole world will seem tragic, because Daddy ate one of the French fries by mistake or because there won't be another reading of *Goodnight Little Owl*. The good enough parent feels sufficiently resourceful not to hold it against the child that it is making a big deal out of so-called 'nothing'. It will follow the child in its excitement over a puddle and in its grief over an uncomfortable sock. It understands that the child's future ability to be considerate to other people and to handle genuine disasters will be critically dependent on having had its fill of sympathy for a range of age-appropriate sorrows.

Forgiveness

A loving parent will know how to put the best possible interpretation on behaviour that might seem to others unfortunate and grating. The small child isn't a 'troublemaker', but it has been upset by the arrival of its sibling. It isn't 'antisocial', but it does find a small circle of familiar people especially soothing. It isn't a 'nightmare', but it certainly does need to go to bed soon. This capacity for imaginative, kindly explanations will go on to mould the workings of the child's own conscience; it will learn the art of self-forgiveness. It won't have to torture itself for its mistakes. It won't suffer the ravages of self-loathing or ever, when it messes up badly, be tempted to take its own life.

Strange phases
The loving parent will feel sufficiently sane to allow a child to be weird for a while, knowing that so-called 'weirdness' is part of normal development. It won't get flustered that the child has decided to pretend it is an animal or wants to eat only red-coloured foods or has an imaginary friend living in the tree at the end of the garden. The adult will have faith in sanity emerging, and in the wisdom of exploring a lot of possible options before choosing to settle on reason. It will be able to remain calm over some intense tantrums and obsessions; it won't need to shut down irreverence at every turn; it will be patient around low moods and unruffled by adolescent surliness. It will know how many byways of strange or unfortunate behaviour one

might need to linger in before being able to accede to a realistic adulthood. Along the way, the parent won't assign labels to the child that might fix it in a role it was only trying out. It will be wary of telling a child that it is 'the angry one', 'the little philosopher' or even 'the kind one': it will allow the child the luxury of picking its own identity.

Clinginess

The good parent knows that children may cling for a long while, and will never dismiss this natural need for reassurance in pejorative terms. It won't tell the child to buck up and be a 'good little man' or a 'young lady who can make me proud'. It will know that those who end up securely attached and able to tolerate absence are those who were originally allowed to have as much dependence and connection as they needed. There will be few requests to be 'brave' at the school gates.

Money

No matter how much money a loving parent might have, it won't ask the child to be grateful and believe that it has a 'privileged' life just because there are foreign holidays, two shiny new cars in the drive and a cleaner. Nor will a more disadvantaged parent fear that a child is damned because the finances are tight and a trip to the cinema would be a significant treat. The loving parent knows that the only real privilege for a child is to know that it is profoundly wanted.

Perfection

A loving parent won't set themselves up as impossibly glamorous or remote, a figure whom a child might be tempted to idealise and ruminate over from afar. They will know how to be present and ordinary around the house; dignified perhaps, but also on occasion ratty, forgetful, silly and greedy for more dessert. The good parent will know that parental quirks and flaws are there to remind a child to reconcile itself to its own humanity – and also eventually to leave home and get on with its own life.

Boringness

A good parent will know how to appear boring. It will understand that what a child chiefly needs is a source of reliable calm, not fireworks and excitement (it has enough of these inside its own mind). The good parent should be there, in the same place, saying more or less the same things, for decades. It should take care to be predictable and to edit out its surprising moods. The child doesn't need a full picture of every perturbance and temptation coursing through its carers' minds. The parent accepts that 'mummy' and 'daddy' are roles, not full representations; it should be the privilege of every child not to have to know its parents in complete detail.

Unreciprocated love

The good parent isn't looking for a balanced relationship. It is happy to give unilaterally. It doesn't need to be asked how its day was or what it thinks of the government's new policy on insurance. It knows that a child should be able to take a parent substantially for granted. The parents' reward for all their work won't be direct; it will arrive by noting, in many years' time, that their child has developed into a very good parent themselves.

Expectations

Wise parents know that children can wind up mentally unwell not so much because they are ignored or maltreated, but because they are loved with a troubling over-intensity by parents who are using them to compensate for disappointments in their own lives. There are childhoods where, upon arrival, the infant is heralded as profoundly exceptional. It is declared uncommonly beautiful, intelligent, talented and set for a special destiny. Not for this child are the ordinary sorrows and stumblings of an average life. While perhaps still no taller than a bollard, the offspring is spoken of as a figure whose name will reverberate down the centuries.

On the surface, this could seem to offer a route to self-confidence and security. But to place such expectations on someone who still struggles with their coat buttons leaves the child feeling hollow and incapable. It grows up with a latent sense of fraudulence, and a consistent fear that it will be unmasked. It winds up at once expecting that others will recognise its sensational destiny and entirely unsure as to why or how they might do so. The child's underlying longing is not so much to revolutionise nations and be honoured across the ages; it is to be accepted and loved for who it is, in all its often touching but unimpressive and faltering realities.

Humour

A loving household isn't one where there is uncomplicated happiness; it is one where, through parental guidance, different members have learnt to show one another a high degree of forbearance for the profoundly grating behaviours of which they know they are all guilty. For this to be possible, the child will need to have been on the receiving end of parental forgiveness over many years. The parent will need to have been indulgently kind in the face of a thousand frustrations and have passed on the knack of letting an irritant go. Now, everyone in the family can see everyone else as fundamentally silly rather than evil. Dad's neuroticism, Mum's obsessiveness, brother's moodiness and sister's sternness will be matters for amused commentary rather than rage or bitterness. The family will be an exemplar of madness benignly handled and absorbed.

Put simply: love is the considerate, tender, patient behaviour displayed by an adult over many years towards a child who cannot help but be largely out of control, confused, frustrating and bewildered. Over time this will allow the child to grow into an adult who can take its place in society without too much of a loss of spontaneity, without too much terror and with a basic trust in its own capacities and chances of fulfilment.

It should be a matter of global consternation that, despite our many advances, we are still only at the dawn of knowing how to ensure that we all have the loving childhoods we deserve.

3. Lessons in Curiosity

One of the things it is easiest to forget about children is that they are aliens recently descended from another planet. In the way they look at everything around them, in the wide-open stares they give to ways of living and being that have grown familiar and therefore invisible to our eyes, they may as well have just stepped off a galactic craft in an unobserved corner of a wheat field. Coming from so far away, everything on our Earth is to them new, interesting and worthy of examination. Nothing is to be taken for granted. There are so many questions to ask. The whole world is, via their as yet unmarked minds, born anew.

In a more limited way, we know from our experiences of travelling how much, in an unfamiliar country, we suddenly notice and are stimulated by. A scene that leaves the locals unimpressed will appear to us filled with wonder and surprise. Shortly after landing in a new place, we might head out into the bustling streets of the capital. We might spot a man in a barbershop and reflect on how extraordinary the shaving ritual looks here, staring at it in fascination from a traffic island and being almost run down by a family on a scooter in the process. There might be a cave-like shop displaying hundreds of different sorts of nuts and spices of a variety we had never guessed existed. Across a stall, two women might be engaged in a passionate discussion about a famous local singer whose stellar career and colourful love life we had never suspected. By a pomegranate juice stand, a man might be reading a newspaper and we can imagine what roiling political events might have provoked the flowing, curling words of the headline splashed across the front.

A little time in this new realm hints at priorities and concerns completely detached from our own. The foreign land is a symbol of a basic idea: that the world is so much bigger and more mysterious than we suppose day to day, that what we know comprises only a tiny part of what there is, and that there is hence never a good excuse for feeling overly bored or imagining that we understand much of anything.

Travellers aside, the other group who cannot forget how surprising, beautiful and worthy of deep examination everything is, are artists. The basic precondition of being an artist is not so much that one knows how to draw, sculpt or photograph; it's that one insists on being amazed. Think of Albrecht Dürer at the start of the 16th century, already 35 years old, but looking at hands as though he had never seen any before. He

Albrecht Dürer, *Study of Three Hands*, c. 1490–1494

appreciates with some of the intensity of a visitor from planet Kepler-22b in the constellation of Cygnus the bizarreness of how fingers interlace, how foldable they are, in what varied shapes and textures they come, how different the skin can be on a thumb compared to an index finger, how expressive a knuckle can be and what wonders of complex geometry lie in a folded palm.

Or think of the American photographer William Eggleston, his attention detained in a café somewhere in suburbia not by any overtly grand political event or high-status local, but by the sight of a condiment

William Eggleston, *Untitled*, c. 1983–1986

display on a table. A small bottle of Tabasco illuminated by a shaft of light reveals itself as a near-transcendent object around which more pious societies might have chosen to found a new religion; a bottle of pickles emerges from his lens as no less awe-inspiring than a specimen jar containing the limbs of a long-deceased leviathan of the deep in the vaults of a natural history museum.

Like artists and travellers, only more so, small children cannot see anything as 'normal'. They spot the button on our jacket and ask themselves: what is this dazzling object (easily as interesting as a light switch or my toes)? What enables it to stay where it is? What would it taste like? What would happen if one struck it with a knife? How would it respond to being coated in apple sauce? Might it make a noise if one blew through the four little holes at its centre? How strongly might it resist a tug? Then there is a pencil: by what mysterious combination of elements does this contraption appear to leak out a grey line when pressed against paper, but lets out very little when pushed against a blanket or a sister's cheek? Does it matter what direction one holds it up in? What would happen if one threw it across the room or dropped it quietly in the sink?

All the great scientific discoveries and works of art have been made by people who looked at things with the naïvety of children; conversely, all the world-weariness has been the result of decades-old humans allowing habit to get in the way of astonishment.

The problem with children is that their curiosity can be too rampant, undisciplined and at odds with what we're trying to get done, so we might end up wishing there was less of it and a bit more apathy and muteness. We're also quite tired. Irritated, we say that it is just the way it is and has always been and could you please, please get a move on. It can feel more important to make it to the shops to pick up a magazine than to stay rooted in one spot for over four minutes, staring at a weed growing out of a wall as if we were a 19th-century explorer investigating the flora of Ecuador's Chimborazo volcano. But we thereby send out a message that being curious and poking at the apparent 'normality' of things is not a particularly estimable activity. If a child wants to be like us one day, a respectable impressive adult, they should be rather less amazed and rather keener to get on with their day.

The tension often comes to the fore around vacuuming. The child is, understandably, dazzled. A machine the size of two pillows is letting out a thunderous sound. At the end of a slightly squashy hose, something is sucking in air with terrifying but also mesmerising force. You can put some car keys thirty centimetres away from the hose and they'll start to move across the carpet and promptly disappear with a fascinating

Hoover advertisement, 1950s

clink-clunk-clink-boom sound into the bowels of the machine. Then there's a button you can press and the entire tangled cable to which the beast is fixed to the wall goes taut and yanks back the contraption as if it were a furious dog on a leash. The child is as transfixed as the most beatific early customer in an advert from the 1950s – an era when wonder was still allowed, in this domain at least. However, this is hardly the state of mind of the busy parent, cursing housework, without much energy to contemplate young Alexander von Humboldt or Michael Faraday tinkering on the carpet beside them.

Much the same dynamic is likely to be repeated around aeroplanes. How bored we are of these dirty machines and how revolted we are by airports. How weary we've become of cabin announcements and moving maps, of inflight trays and safety cards; how cold our hearts are to the sight of the engines slung beneath those long flexible wings, powering us over small puffy clouds like those in the backdrop of a Piero della Francesca altarpiece. But the child has correctly apprised that nothing up here is normal and isn't about to let go of their fascination, even if it means letting out a scream or two. From an opposing window seat, William Eggleston understands only too well.

William Eggleston, *Untitled*, 1971–1974

We sometimes ask ourselves what the Romans might have made of our modern bathrooms, or what a medieval knight might have made of a shopping centre or a telephone. We can more accurately ask ourselves what the first man or woman to emerge from Africa's Rift Valley would have thought of our lives – because we have our own version of this early hominid right to hand in the cot.

Every new human provides our species with a chance to return to first principles and rethink everything from the ground up. We should allow the child to ask its questions and to pop as many things as safely possible into its mouth. And when one can't say why or how, rather than look cross or bored, we should say that we'll find out together. We could keep a list of topics of enquiry somewhere in the kitchen: how car indicators make that sound, why trees bud in spring, how clouds move, how long it would take for sheep to grow back their wool and why Granny looks a bit cross whenever Dad is in the room. A child's greatest gift to us is to keep insisting that nothing is ever normal.

4. Lessons in Soothing

One of the greatest skills any parent can possess is a capacity for soothing. In a better arranged society, we would celebrate not only gifted athletes and canny entrepreneurs, but also those gentle souls who are most effective at delivering reassurance to their frightened offspring.

In premodern societies, the need for parental-style soothing was well understood at a collective level. In Christianity, the faithful turned to their primordial soothing figure, Mother Mary, who knew about suffering, who would listen to our sorrows and extend her sympathy at moments of dread and panic. In a comparable spirit, Buddhists would turn to the figure of Guanyin, a female deity with a sound sense of the difficulties involved in trying to survive and a ready supply of sweetness and compassion.

Giovanni Bellini, *Madonna of the Meadow*, 1505

Guanyin statue, China, Northern Song Dynasty, c. 1025

Soothing is now principally left to parents. One might propose that there is nothing more important required of a parent than a capacity to soothe, this being the skill to which all other parental capabilities ultimately point.

Here are some of the things a parent gifted at soothing will know how to do:

Identify that soothing is required

Not everyone who needs to be soothed is aware of the fact or grateful to be reminded of their vulnerability. Some of those who would most benefit from soothing present as angry, defiant and aggressive; it looks as though soothing would be the last thing on their minds. But the soother looks beneath this independent bluster and insists on kindness nonetheless. They know that every case of nastiness or haughtiness, cynicism or viciousness contains a disguised longing for love. The truly soothing person is canny and generous enough to keep gifting assistance even to those prickly, wounded souls who need kindness so badly that they have forgotten how to ask for it.

Normalise the need

The good soother subtly indicates that a search for soothing is 'normal', respectable and dignified.

They know that life is constantly at risk of overwhelming even the most capable of humans, and that there is nothing shameful about seeking assistance. Not being able to cope doesn't require special permission; nor does the problem need to be vast. One might need soothing simply because one is feeling sad and it's a cold, dark Sunday evening. A good parental soother teaches a child to have an unembarrassed relationship to their own vulnerability, helping to stamp out the pressure to pretend to be stronger than one is that invariably ends up making one weaker and lesser than one should be.

Some people might worry that offering too much soothing to a child risks turning them into malingering attention-seekers. We might reply that attention-seekers are never people who have had too much attention; they are people the world tragically forgot existed. No one who has been properly and consistently soothed will spend their adult life in desperate bids to be noticed; the most logical outcome for a child who has been well soothed will be to devote energy to soothing other people.

Holding

Touch is a primary weapon against distress. At the news of anxiety, the soother doesn't hesitate to hold the other person tightly in their arms, giving them a visceral sense of being a protective figure who is on their side against their foes. The panicked breathing and racing heartbeat have a chance to align with the steadier rhythms of the soothing party. In the early days, a soother might place an infant on their shoulder and stroke their head and back. Later on, it might be a cuddle on a knee, and later still, a standing hug. But the message will remain the same: the suffering will not have to be borne alone.

Singing

Lullabies reveal the extent to which it is not necessarily words that can make us feel more tranquil. The baby doesn't understand what's being said, but they are calmed all the same by even the clumsiest (but most heartfelt) song; this shows us that we are tonal creatures long before we are creatures of understanding.

Ancient Greek mythology was fascinated by the story of the musician Orpheus, who had to rescue his wife from the underworld. To get there he needed to make his way past Cerberus, a ferocious three-headed dog that

Orpheus demonstrating the power of music by soothing
Cerberus with his lyre.

guarded the entrance to the land of the dead. Orpheus
was said to have played such sweet, enchanting music
that the wild beast calmed down and became mild
and docile. The Greeks were reminding themselves
of the psychological power of music. Orpheus didn't
reason with Cerberus; he didn't try to explain how

important it was that he should be allowed to pass; he didn't speak about how much he loved his wife and how much he wanted her back. Cerberus was pretty much immune to reason – as we ourselves are in times of distress. But he was still open to being soothed. It was a matter of finding the right channel to reach him: the medium of music.

Concern

At the first mention of an ailment, the good soother puts into motion some well-practised responses: most importantly, a suggestion that one lie down on the sofa (for challenges should never be faced in a vertical position for too long), then be given a blanket (probably oversized, thick and a bit worn) and, afterwards, a hand on the forehead to check for a raised temperature. Soon after, it might be time for a tray with a drink and a slice of cake.

Food

Hunger isn't the point; it's the idea of nourishment that counts. The good soother will at once offer a range of dishes: hot chocolate for sure, but also toast, lemon cake and perhaps a soft-boiled egg. The rituals of preparation are central; familiar smells should come from the kitchen along with the gentle knocking of pans and crockery, active symbols of concern and kindly bustle.

In one of the most soothing paintings in the world, the 18th-century French artist Jean-Baptiste-Siméon Chardin shows us a woman in a plain kitchen taking the top off a boiled egg. The title of the painting, *The Attentive Nurse*, lets us know that the food is destined for someone who is unwell, but cleverly, Chardin has kept this figure out of sight. Here he intends to celebrate the carer rather than the cared for. He wants us to notice the qualities of patience, concentration and genial concern in the woman. We are being reminded of what love involves and how deeply indebted we are – all of us who enjoy a measure of health and sanity – to those who once soothed and ministered to us.

Nicknames

The good soother renames their youngest charges during their difficulties. Like a patient in a hospital whose wrist is ringed with an identifying code upon registration, so too is the soother's offspring assigned a new name for the duration of the crisis. Ideally this name indicates both smallness and bravery, vulnerability and strength: 'sweet soldier' or 'brave mushroom' perhaps, or 'gutsy button' or 'poor potpot' (alliterations are

Jean-Baptiste-Siméon Chardin, *The Attentive Nurse* or *The Nourishment of Convalescence*, 1747

especially good). This might be supplemented with the word 'my' to imply – like a general with his troops – that one is very much fighting this together, be it a virus or a bout of sadness.

Being boring

The most soothing people are a little boring, in a good way. We aren't looking to them to entertain us or dazzle us in our moments of woe. While a crisis lasts, we just need them to be pottering around quietly, realigning books or sorting out the photos, and telling us a few simple things about local life: what's going on with the neighbour's rabbit, what the lady in the post office said about her son's exam results. This is not a time for big ambitions or perplexing theories; we're retrenching and can be cheered by nothing larger than a short walk around the park or the sight of a vase of pretty spring flowers. The normal horizons and ambitions have fallen away and we're taking it a day – or a few hours – at a time.

Loyalty

The good soother leaves us in no doubt as to where their loyalties lie. We don't even need to have finished recounting our mistreatment at the hands of others for them to be ready with their outraged interventions on our behalf: *what absolute cheek! They need their head examined! What a monster! If they dare to lay a hand on you, I'm going to* ... Normally gentle souls reveal they have a backbone – and more. They would fight to the death for us. They are suddenly fearsome combatants and would risk their life for us. They don't expect us to be perfect – we might be to blame as well – but for now they are wholeheartedly on our side. It's the way they are built. They may respect the law in theory, but in principle they'd do pretty much anything to spring us out of prison.

A household in which soothing manoeuvres unfold sets a child up for life. It won't then matter what troubles they encounter; they will be armed with the finest psychological weapons with which to slay them. Even better, the soothing voice won't merely be a voice outside of them; it will become the way they speak to themselves. Years later, when the soothing parent might no longer be with them, and time might have greyed and aged them, they will still be able to minister to their own needs with the tenderness they learnt in their long-distant childhood; they'll know that the storm will pass, especially if they find a way to have a lie down and, perhaps, a boiled egg.

5. Lessons in Listening

The suggestion that parents might not be listening hard enough to their children will strike the average mother or father as, at best, maddening and, at worst, simply cruel. After all, a central part of the parental experience is likely to be noise: a continuous soundtrack of cries, exclamations, demands, shrieks, questions and tantrums. The chances of finishing a quiet sentence, let alone a paragraph, are negligible for many years. To insinuate that one might not be listening seems like an absurd taunt designed to erode away any last vestige of sanity.

Yet, despite having had to put up with unholy degrees of noise, one might still be missing the signal. Indeed, there might be a cacophony in the household precisely because the signal keeps getting lost. Things have grown noisy because, somewhere in the mix, someone feels as if they are not being heard.

This is hardly anyone's fault. The one thing children cannot be expected to do from the outset is speak clearly and accurately about what ails them. They hardly understand their own minds, let alone those of others. With only the barest grasp of what they are experiencing, they have no chance of imparting news of their emotions to those around them in a way that might convince or alert an exhausted or busy adult. Their communication styles veer between the frustrating and the plain frightening. They can be:

Violent:	*I wish Granny would die ...*
	Baby should go in the bin.
Hurtful:	*You only ever think about yourself ...*
	You're boring.
Mean-spirited:	*Yasmin is disgusting.*
Rebellious:	*I'm never ever going back to school.*
Illogical:	*I don't care if we've come to Spain,*
	I hate it here.
Irrational:	*I only want Daddy to open my*
	yogurt pot.

If parents occasionally shut their ears, it's not because they are mean; it's because what is being said comes across as such a violation of their hopes for their offspring – and human nature more broadly. It can seem as though, after extraordinary sacrifices on their part, these parents have managed to produce a being who is spoilt, ungrateful, fussy, depressive and odd. It isn't so much that the parents haven't heard; it's more that they are hoping that what's been said isn't really true, particularly if it's batted away swiftly and blithely. This explains the archetypal way in which parents don't listen: they swerve away from the message being proferred to them in favour of imploring a child to be more sensible or, to put it crudely, 'more normal'. The following might occur:

Child: *I'm feeling sad.*
Parent: *Don't be silly, you can't be – it's the holidays.*

Child: *I'm really worried.*
Parent: *That's ridiculous, there's nothing to be scared of here.*

Child: *I wish there wasn't any school ever ever.*
Parent: *Don't be difficult. You know we have to leave the house by 8.*

Child: *I can't bear Sam, he's so silly.*
Parent: *Now that's not a nice thing to say – Sam is your little brother!*

To repeat: it isn't that the parent is unable to hear what is being said; it's fear – fear that the child is saying something that doesn't fit an understanding of what is considered 'normal'. The parent is scared by evidence that the child is manifesting emotions or behaviours that will make their future difficult: that they might become a child murderer, an arsonist, a depressive, a neurotic, a scaredy-cat or a delinquent. They worry that their beloved child might become someone who has a problem with authority or who never gets a job, whose life is ruined by unnatural exigencies or marred by excessive revulsions. That's why these parents are not in a mood calmly to listen to plots to kill Granny or never to return to school, to listen to searing disappointment about the colour of the icing or terrors about a jungle animal lurking under the sofa. It isn't that they don't care; it's just that they're anxious about who their child might be turning out to be.

This suggests a route out of the problem. It isn't about not listening *per se*; it's first and foremost about a parent's relationship to so-called normality. It's about broadening one's sense of this state to encompass a far broader range of behaviours than one might previously have considered. Sanity has a lot of room in it for madness, so, when considered with sufficient imagination, it can be quite normal for us to be so angry with people that we think of wanting to kill them, or that we can adore someone and at the same time wish they could go into the bin. Listening is about having the inner confidence to allow a child to be a bit weird, a bit contrary, a bit frustrating and a bit lost; all of these belong to health and ordinary development.

A parent more reconciled to the 'abnormality' of sanity would have time for some properly unusual news emanating from the younger generation. They would feel that they could calmly listen to unconventional statements without the foundations of civilisation caving in. In response to certain messages, they might answer with equanimity:

- 'Maybe you were really hoping Granny would be able to come to your birthday. I think we would all have wanted her to be here ...'

- 'I'm hearing that I've annoyed you a lot in some way. I'm not sure how, but I love you deeply and maybe you'll be able to tell me in a little bit ...'

- 'You're very annoyed you have a baby brother now and everyone fusses over him. I felt that way when

Auntie Jane was born – though I'm pretty good friends with her now. Maybe you will get on with Sam one day. But that's a long way away now.'

The more we listen to the 'weird' messages that children send us, the less furiously they will have to make them. We've all had the experience, when faced with someone who has not heard us, of amping up what we have to say, whether in volume, urgency or intensity. The more *we* listen, the quieter *they* can be. A child who says they want to burn the school down doesn't want to burn the school down; they want to be heard for the deep frustration that school is causing them. They will only become an arsonist if we continue not to listen – not if we do so amply and with tolerant good humour.

Similarly, take a child who has been flown to Spain at considerable expense and yet says, at the beach on the first day, that they don't like it here and wish they were home. They won't grow into a spoilt ingrate if one takes the trouble to ask them why they're feeling sad; if one can be robust enough about one's parenting capacities to get down on one knee and ask, 'Tell me more about why you don't want to be here?' The child just wants a chance to share their discombobulation, their excitement and their fear at their own excitement. They want to hear that their feelings at the surprisingness of being far from home by the sea can be confirmed by someone they trust. And once they've been heard, they'll almost certainly head into the waves; they'll be interested in the churros and hot chocolate at breakfast; they'll remember to admire the palm trees in the hotel forecourt and the pretty lights by the pool.

We need a chance to feel sad if we're to be able to be authentically happy; we need to be able to say that we want the whole world to die in order gradually to become responsible and kind. What hard-of-hearing parents forget is that feelings, especially difficult feelings, invariably weaken when they've been aired. Feelings get less strong, not stronger, as soon as they've been recognised. We scream when no one has listened, not when they have listened amply with care.

Imaginative listening is at the heart of what love is and involves. We might define love as a willingness to go beneath the surface of what someone is saying – which might be abrupt, perplexing or brutal – in order to locate a deeper meaning or intention, which is almost certainly more benevolent and more worthy of sympathetic consideration. This holds true as much in adult relationships as in parent–child ones. When we say that we hate a partner's guts, it's almost never the case that we do; we seldom say stark, vicious things to people unless we love them a lot. It is usually a sign of immense hope that has been dashed or shaken. We don't hate our partner; we hate having to depend on them. We are scared that they hold the keys to our happiness. What we are truly trying to say to them is: 'I'm scared that I love you so much and that you can rattle me so easily.' It is a paradox of the human brain that such an emotion may come out as: 'Go away and die.'

In this respect, listening well to another person may mean taking them seriously, while not necessarily sticking only to the surface of their words. 'I hate you' may mean 'I love you'; 'I don't care' may mean 'I'm very scared'. Something important may be being said to us, but its full meaning may be to the side of the words that have actually been uttered. We might, along with listening, need to do a bit of translating.

Many foreign languages feature what translators call 'false friends' – words that strongly suggest they mean one thing when they mean another. The Italian word *baldo* sounds to an English speaker as if it must mean 'bald', whereas it actually means 'brave'. The French word *monnaie* can seem as if it must mean 'money', when it in fact refers to loose change. One of the key steps to successfully learning a foreign language is to get used to discounting the 'obvious' implications of certain words and to work harder at determining their true meaning.

We need to practise something similar around children. Here, too, a foreign language can be involved and 'false friends' are rife: words and phrases where the meaning is not what we might initially suppose and where we need a dictionary to help us with the critical task of translation. In the ideal future, we will have in our ears little devices that will translate children's words into what they actually mean. We will hear (via our discreet, brushed steel appliances) not what they say overtly, but what they are attempting to communicate. Ideally, they would be wearing one too, because the challenge of translation is always mutual.

Until that time, though, we will have to rely on vigilance. When a child says something that violates our sense of normality, we should refrain from shutting things down and simply respond: 'Wow, tell me more ...' When we've heard a strong but surprising declaration ('The baby should be buried alive ...'), we should dare to say: 'Maybe what you want to say is ...' When they declare: 'I hate you all', rather than retort: 'It's bad to be angry', we might look unruffled and remark: 'I can see you must be frustrated ...' At the same time, we should note how often, despite being around our children, we have managed not to let their full reality into our consciousness, how often we have taken in one of their feelings and too quickly redescribed it as illegitimate, inaccurate or unacceptable.

One of the deepest of all human wishes is that other people should listen to what it feels like to be us. We might add: we don't necessarily need them to agree with all our feelings or follow up on them, but what we crave is that they take time to hear them. The more we have been heard, the quieter we can be. Most so-called bad behaviour on the part of children isn't that at all. It is an unhelpful but understandable response to not being heard for what they have not yet been able to say clearly or diplomatically.

6. Lessons in Melancholy

It is an axiom of modern parenting that a good childhood should, first and foremost, be a happy childhood. This means that there should be smiles from the start. No sooner has a baby found out how to control its own mouth than it should be up for games of peekaboo. Visitors who pick it up and give it a friendly cuddle expect to be rewarded with at least a few bouts of giggling. At nursery, small children who have just been dropped off by their parents for the day will be asked to sing, clap their hands and dance in unison in celebration of jolly themes, many related to farmyard animals – and may be singled out as unusual if they don't manage a degree of ardour that would put a dictator's independence day celebrations to shame.

Then there are the birthdays, key occasions to celebrate the joys of being alive, when parents and relatives strain every sinew to ensure that the child will display appropriate evidence of delight. The jollity extends to the visual atmosphere of childhood: primary colours, bold brushstrokes, bright cartoonish faces – and an absence of charcoal greys or muted greens. To cap the impression, advertising is certain that any child fit to appear on a screen or a billboard must be an exuberant one, touched to the core by the discovery of a new kind of corn-syrup-infused cereal or trans-fat-rich mid-morning snack.

Ritz magazine advert, 1950s

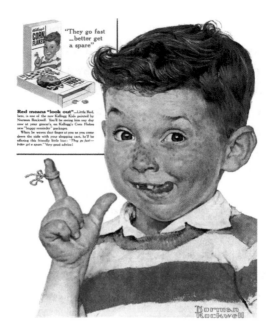

Kellogg's Corn Flakes advertisement, illustrated by Norman
Rockwell, 1955

But all this jolliness leaves aside a crucial truth that
adults wilfully ignore when it comes to children: every
life, even a very good one, is filled with challenges
that warrant regret, anxiety, grief and feelings of loss.
Sadness is not an anomaly; it is an apt and appropriate
response to the tragedy of being alive. One should not
have to worry that someone is sad; one would need to be
alarmed if they didn't know how to be sad sometimes.

It is sometimes suggested that childhood is 'easier' than adulthood, and therefore sunnier, because children do not yet have to pay a mortgage or work in an office. But this is to forget how much small people have on their plates from the start. First comes the definitive loss of one's first home, the womb, and its incomparable convenience and cosiness. Then a baby has to adjust to the incessant frustrations of the early weeks and months in a brightly lit, harsh world. They suffer being wet and cold without any understanding of why or how; they might have a sore scalp, dry skin, a burp that will not come, a stricken sense of being uncomfortably bloated and full, a colon that does not yet properly function, an irritating ray of sunshine that is blinding them but that no one else has spotted, an inability to do anything but scream when it might want to share so many nuanced and subtle thoughts, long nights when it feels bereft of touch and lies marooned and helpless for what can feel like a century, wailing its lungs out from panic and finally falling asleep in sobs of uncontained distress at its apparently permanent abandonment.

In the day come spoons full of unfamiliar and often distasteful foods, then constant bouts of socialising with other confusing babies it is meant to find interesting. At all times, the parents it adores are in danger of finding better things to do. Maddeningly, they seem to have friends of their own that they love to see. They might even have another child, a source of distress no less great than is an affair in an adult relationship. A child might be, historically speaking, in a privileged position; there might not be a war or a food shortage. But still, there are so many toys it can't have, car journeys that don't end, drums and cymbals it's meant to love hitting, endless school with its strange smells and bizarre teachers, the meanness of other children, the arguments of its parents, the siblings it fears or resents … And to think that, on top of all this, it is expected to smile.

A good childhood is not a cheery one; it is one where a young person is allowed to feel real, which is a far greater and more useful achievement. This might mean that one regularly has a chance to have a good cry and lose all hope. Or that one can sit and look at the rain fall and be deeply regretful and bleak. Or that one can refuse to put one's hands together and clap, given that Mummy won't be back for another five hours.

Applying pressure on someone to be content when there is no authentic reason to be so is not kindness. It is a form of well-meaning coercion that forces a child to lose connection with their own reality and to distance themselves from an honest relationship with who they actually are. True care for a child should mean allowing them to have their own feelings. These might include some giggling and heartfelt delight, but could also involve resentment, moroseness, hopelessness, sorrow and dejection – all legitimate responses to the world as it is. One should not worry about an occasionally sad child; one would have to worry about a child who had been given no other option than to smile.

The most smile-sensitive parents in the history of humanity were those of an Indian prince called Siddhārtha Gautama, known to us now as the Buddha, who was born in the 5th century BCE in Lumbini, Nepal. Legend tells us that the Buddha's parents decided that his childhood should be entirely happy: all references to sadness or grief were banished and the prince was surrounded only by evidence of happiness and health, bountifulness and beauty. But the Buddha sensed that he was being shielded from important truths and, stifled by the denial, eventually slipped out from the palace to discover what the world was actually like. His response made its way into the philosophy of Buddhism. This reminds us in categorical terms – in its first and most important tenet – that 'life is suffering'. Paradoxically, Buddhism is a joyful creed, but the joy is not of the sentimental kind that denies that pain exists. It is the joy that springs forth with particular vigour once one has a proper measure of how difficult things really are; it is the determined joy of those who have squared up to misery and are all the more alive to the converse.

A place for sadness is especially key in adolescence, when a child not only has an unparalleled range of issues to deal with, but might also be coming under particular pressure not to be morose. What allows parents to tolerate their teenager's sadness is, ultimately, a proper confrontation with their own sources of grief. They may need to acknowledge, first to themselves and then the wider family, how much they regret and are sometimes at sea, how little they understand and how vulnerable they can feel. Strangely, the result won't be to drag the other members of the family down; it will be to give children vital role models for how to accept their own darker emotions and respond to them without shame or fear. The kindest thing a parent might do for a child is to admit that feelings of sorrow and confusion lie at the heart of a good enough and responsible adult life. We should never, like the kindly Gautamas, be tempted to educate our children to expect a world that does not exist.

Put another way, the happiest families are those that know how to be melancholy when the situation demands it. Melancholy is not rage or bitterness; it is a noble species of sadness that arises when we are open to the fact that life is inherently difficult for everyone and that suffering and disappointment are at the heart of all experience. Melancholy springs from a rightful awareness of the tragic structure of our lives. We can, in melancholy states, understand without fury or sentimentality that understanding other people is hard, that loneliness is universal and that every life has its measure of shame and sorrow.

The dominant cheery tone of many familial relationships falsely presumes that the best way to please others is to present ourselves in a vibrant mood, when in fact, admission of our despair, and of the number of moments when we wonder if it can really be worth it, are key tools in the process of kindness properly reimagined. The jollying parent is driven by a compulsion to impose a mood that has no basis in reality. The jollier doesn't just want the child to be happy; they can't tolerate the idea that it might be sad, so unexplored, unresolved and potentially overwhelming are their own feelings of disappointment.

Childhood is necessarily full of sadness (as adulthood is too), which means we must be granted permission to have periods of mourning: for a broken toy, the grey sky or perhaps the lingering sadness we can see in our parents' eyes. The good carer needs to remember how much of life deserves solemn and mournful states, and how much love we will feel for those who aren't aggressively compelled to deny our tears. The more melancholy a family can be, the less its individual members need to be persecuted by their own failures, lost illusions and regrets.

Across history, the articulation of melancholic attitudes in works of art has provided us with relief from a sense of loneliness and persecution. Among others, Lady Murasaki, John Keats, Percy Bysshe Shelley, Arthur Schopenhauer, Virginia Woolf, Joan Didion and Joni Mitchell have been able to reassure us of the normalcy of our states of sadness. It's a pity that so few works of art have featured melancholy children.

The few examples that exist show us how valuable such art could be, demonstrating that children don't always have to be smiling or celebrating, but can also be distant, lost in their thoughts and sizing up the world for the pains it will deliver them.

Ferdinand Hodler, *Portrait of Louise Delphine Duchosal*, 1885

It isn't an insult to us or a sign that we have failed our children if we sometimes find them in their rooms disconsolate and in tears. It could be a sign that we have been brave enough to allow them to understand life on their own terms.

7. Lessons in Naughtiness

Imagine two different kinds of family, each around their own dinner table on a typical evening.

In Family One, the child is well behaved. They say how nice the food is, they talk about what happened at school, they listen to what their parents have on their minds and at the end they go off to finish their homework.

In Family Two, things are rather different. The child calls their mother an idiot; they snort with derision when their father says something; they make a rude comment that reveals a lack of embarrassment about their body; if the parents ask how their homework is going, they say school is stupid and they storm off and slam the door.

It looks as if everything is going well in Family One and badly in Family Two. But if we look inside the child's mind we might get a different picture. In Family One, the so-called 'good' child has a whole range of emotions inside them that they keep out of sight, not because they want to, but because they don't feel they have the option to be tolerated as they really are. They feel they can't let their parents see if they are angry or fed up or bored because it seems as if the parents have no inner resources to cope with their reality; they must repress their bodily, coarse, more volatile selves. Any criticism of a grown-up is (they imagine) so wounding and devastating that it can't be uttered.

In Family Two, the so-called 'bad' child knows that things are robust. They feel they can tell their mother she's a useless idiot because they know that she loves them and that they love her and that a bout of irritated stroppiness won't damage anything. They know their father won't fall apart or take revenge for being mocked. The environment is warm and strong enough to absorb the child's aggression, anger, dirtiness or disappointment.

As a result, there's an unexpected outcome: the good child is heading for problems in adult life, typically to do with excessive compliance, rigidity, lack of creativity and an unbearably harsh conscience that might spur on suicidal thoughts. Meanwhile, the naughty child is on the way to healthy maturity, which comprises spontaneity, resilience, a tolerance of failure and a sense of self-acceptance.

What we call naughtiness is really an early exploration of authenticity and independence. As former naughty children, we can be more creative because we can try out ideas that don't instantly meet with approval; we can make a mistake or a mess or look ridiculous and it won't be a disaster. Things can be repaired or improved. Our sexuality is essentially acceptable to us, so we don't have to feel excessively humiliated or awkward about introducing it to a partner. We can hear criticisms of ourselves and bear to explore their truths and reject their malice.

We should learn to see naughty children, a few chaotic scenes and occasional raised voices as belonging to health rather than delinquency – and conversely learn to fear small people who cause no trouble whatsoever. If we have occasional moments of happiness and well-being, we should feel especially grateful that there was almost certainly someone in the distant past who opted to look through the eyes of love at some unreasonable and unpleasant behaviour from us.

8. Lessons in Sweetness

If there is one generalisation we can hazard around children, it is that they come across as 'sweet' – on a good day, at least. Their attitudes, mannerisms, games, smiles and ways of curling up in bed at night all point in this direction. Although the idea of sweetness might seem to lie at the more trite or sentimental end of childhood, the term captures a range of important values that might fruitfully be investigated and untangled. We might dare to ask why childhood sweetness sometimes touches us so much, especially at this point in history, and how an encounter with sweetness could help us to reconsider neglected aspects of our own psyches.

We can start in Washington, D.C. in 1961, in the Department of Justice, in the office of Robert F. Kennedy, the US Attorney General. Alongside pictures of the navy from the government's art collection, Kennedy chose to hang a selection of drawings made by his then young children. These works showed docile animals, vast flowers, implausible spaceships and the antics of a gang of siblings.

Robert F. Kennedy in his office, surrounded by his children's drawings, 1961

For almost all of human history, it would have been unthinkable for anyone laying claim to any sort of decorum or sanity to pin a picture by some 4- and 6-year-olds on the walls of their office or throne room.

But the art that people are drawn to – at an individual and collective level – reflects much about what is missing from their lives. The particular register of emotions we're sensitive to in the visual sphere hints at what we long for, but don't reliably have a connection to, in ourselves. In the 19th century, as Britain rapidly industrialised and much of the population moved into cities, there was an explosion of interest in paintings of rural scenes – especially

John Constable, *A Cottage in a Cornfield*, 1817

depictions of shepherds, cottages and lush fields grazed by peaceful cattle. People living in crowded, polluted and busy streets wanted to hang on their walls evocations of vistas they no longer so securely possessed in their souls.

Likewise, as northern Europe became ever more regimented and morally less permissive over the century, so people felt drawn to a kind of art that depicted economically undeveloped societies, especially those of the Middle East, which seemed redolent of an 'exoticism' and sensual enchantment no longer available in Berlin or London.

The logic guiding Kennedy's aesthetic interest was similar. The job of Attorney General had brought with it exceptional responsibilities and obligations: days of meetings where extreme discipline had to be maintained, where hugely consequential decisions were taken – and where no one would especially have appreciated small talk or banter. No wonder that Kennedy might have longed for his eye occasionally to encounter a different atmosphere in which there was room for spontaneity, honesty and idealism. Like many art lovers, Kennedy was seeking in pictures some of what was no longer so available in his life.

Eugène Delacroix, *The Women of Algiers*, 1834

Kennedy was typical of his time. The modern age has become especially interested in children's vivacity, lack of guile, energy and defencelessness – qualities that we group together under the term 'sweet'. What seems to touch us in children are elements that are particularly under threat in adult lives but that we unconsciously recognise as precious to our sense of balance and psychological wholeness. The 'sweet' is a vital part of ourselves currently in exile.

Societies grow sensitive to things that they are missing. We live in a world of highly complex technology, extreme precision in science, massive bureaucracies, insecurity and intense meritocratic competition. To survive with any degree of success in these conditions, we have to be uncommonly controlled, forward-thinking, reasonable and cautious creatures.

Yet it can be hard to see the nature of our burdens. It is rare to acknowledge that we might need more flights of fancy, more innocent trust, more gleeful disregard of expectations. We find it moving – sweet, in fact – to encounter such things in symbolic forms in the ways of children. By decoding children's sweetness, we have an opportunity to get to know our own needs. In their own way, these small people are bearers of compact manifestos for some of what is most urgently required in the anxious, compromised conditions of modernity.

By examining the 'sweet' behaviour of children, we stand to be reminded of virtues we honour in humans large and small – and might aspire to have more of throughout our adult years.

Honesty

Children are singularly honest about their feelings, and although we might make a good show of looking appalled by certain instances of their candour, we secretly cheer them on for their forthrightness. They tell the self-important guest that he has a boring face and the pretentious restaurant that their apparently healthy salads are a grim mush. They declare the prestigious film overrated and tick off their neighbour for not playing with their daughter enough. They aren't interested in having to seem kinder than they are. 'No, mine,' they will say in their early years with admirable abruptness when another child comes to play with their fire engine. This is all part of the work of reminding us of a raft of important feelings that we have forgotten how to register and unfairly sacrificed on the altar of propriety.

Irresponsibility

We tell them, again and again, that the books belong on the shelves, but what can that matter when it is so interesting to pile them up on the floor or knock them down and hear them tumble with a fascinating thunderclap into a dust-releasing heap? Our lives would be nothing if we had not learnt the art of discipline, but nor are these lives worth enduring if we do not sometimes place our own pleasures at the centre of our plans.

Utopianism

Children are full of schemes: what should be taught at school, what films should be about, how bedtime should happen, how to colonise the Andromeda galaxy, the best way to deal with pigeon droppings, how to live in a cupboard on almost no money – and a thousand other utopian proposals besides. A 5-year-old might muse over supper on how it would be nice to have a career that combined being an astronaut with being a chef for the blind; her sister might plan to keep an elephant in the garden; a boy might say he'd like to marry his older brother; another that he wanted to invent a machine that would allow him to reverse time. Rather than dismissing these ideas as idiotic or impractical, we may be enchanted; our pleasure is a sign that we have grown painfully short of the freedom to imagine the better world we privately long for and somewhere still believe in.

Questions

The questions come thick and fast: why is the sea salty? How did the Earth begin? What would an orangutan look like if you shaved its body? There is nothing uninteresting about such enquiries; they get a bad reputation only because of the poor and hasty way in which they are often answered. The questions of children might frustrate us, but they hint at how clever we could all be if only we knew how to keep probing at reality with innocent determination.

Simple pleasures

Children can upset the customary hierarchy of importance. We buy them an expensive toy, and they prefer the box to its contents. They spend an hour examining a brick wall or a zip. They cannot get enough of trying out the light switch. They bang on a bucket and don't tire of the resonance. They don't mind a bit of repetition; everything is so wondrous. That's why we should read the same book fifteen times over – there is always something new to enjoy in it. They see the funny side of small things that we have long forgotten to notice; for example, that we have ears, and how incongruous and therefore comedic it would be if we tried to put a biscuit or two inside them.

Emotional directness

The traditional assumption in drawing is that being 'good' means paying precise attention to what is in front of us. The artist must learn how to observe the world faithfully, and in order to do so, must put a lot of themselves to one side. However, when children draw, they are – as in other areas of their lives – experts at emotional directness. They tend to be much more interested in what they feel than in what they see. Rather than being painstaking or faithful to objective facts, children let us know about the emotions they experienced on seeing a duck or their teacher, their little brother or the first flowers of spring.

What it looked like   What it felt like

If we want a faithful graphic representation of reality, we could take a photograph. But if we seek a portrait of someone's inner life as they come into contact with the external world – and it can be more interesting to do so – we would be better off revering the raw and wonky masterpieces of the under-5s.

Love

We know we can get hurt in love, and that is why we are so coy and reserved, but no such inhibitions attend small children. They will tell us, with reckless honesty, that their love for us is as deep as the Mariana Trench and as wide as the circumference of Jupiter. They swear that we are the best mummy or daddy in the world – which doesn't mean that they won't be fed up with us again in a minute, but why not share the momentary enthusiasm without compunction or caution? They haven't, like us, grown to expect trouble from every direction. They haven't learnt the dangers of trust or the safety of cynicism. Our tears at their declarations remind us of how much we long to recover faith in one another.

Bravery

It can be moving simply to see the clothes of young children: the impossibly little shoes, socks, jackets or knitted jumpers, so like our own but many magnitudes smaller. The feeling can be more powerful still if these clothes belonged to a long-disappeared young person – a child in a time far from our own.

20th-century child's dress, Amsterdam, 1948

Part of what we may be moved by is a recognition of how small a child is in relation to the obstacles it faces. It must encounter frustration and confusion, sorrow and boredom while no taller than a chair, and with fingers no larger than twigs. Yet this physical vulnerability is sometimes accompanied by bold and brave declarations on their part. They offer to fight any burglars that might appear, or to carry Granny back home if she gets too tired; they tell us that if the money were to run out, they would go out and start a business, or that they would piece us back together again if we died. When they are just learning to speak and might be struggling to open a door, they might bat away an offer of help with a stoic: 'No, me do it all on myself.'

We adults might appear no less incongruous in the face of what we have to deal with, if viewed through a telescope from another planet. We too make daring stands against insuperable forces; our whole lives are gambles against impossible odds and almost certain defeats – which we nevertheless largely refuse to contemplate or be worn down by. We call children sweet in the way they attack their challenges, but sweet is how we must appear to the eyes of the gods, contemplating the arduous struggles of our Lilliputian species, building cities and writing books, putting up hospitals and running elections, buoyed by ambitions but destined to oblivion.

The interplay between bravery and suffering is never more apparent than in children who become ill or die before adulthood. If we were really focused on the poignancy of the human condition, we might cry without end at the sight of Alfred Owens, aged 10 months, who died in early March 1868 – and whose serious and determined expression bears testimony to a courage that was no match for the unjust horrors he faced.

Alfred Owens, aged 10 months, 1868

There is nothing petty or sentimental about the sweetness we locate in children. Adults too are as sweet, if we only knew how to detect the quality in them. It is a sign of progress that we have gradually learnt to see the sweetness in children; it will be further progress still when adults more reliably learn to see the sweetness in one another.

9. Lessons in Siblings

One of the most unhelpful things that parents can do is encourage their children to love their siblings – and tell them that it would be 'normal' and a sign of decency for them to do so. They point out – sometimes rather impatiently – how nice the sibling is, how kind and clever it seems, how worthy a creature it will prove. They get cross with the disgruntled child's protests; they come down hard on any signs of loathing and equate virtue with sibling harmony. They might even add how much they, in their wisdom many decades back, happened to love Uncle Yorgos or Auntie Alice. In the process, they make it much harder for children to love their siblings.

We should recognise and honour a basic fact: all things being equal, a sibling is a disaster. It's annoying, it divides the attention, it smells, it doesn't do what one wants and it takes away the light. A sibling is to childhood what an adulterous lover is to a marriage. It's not good news – and as always with things that aren't good news, the best way to handle them is to admit with utter directness how awful they really are.

School is awful and one should be allowed to say so. Grandad can be awful, and that's fine to mention (out of earshot). Daddy is awful at points, and that's OK too. Mummy can be dreadful as well. We never teach a person to love anyone or anything by coercing them into seeing only their upsides.

So, for as long as is necessary, we should take our cue from our child about what a disaster the sibling is. Not egg them on in their hatred – that would be peculiar – nor develop their thinking around their displeasure, but listen, endure the protest and accept the pain they are expressing. It isn't nice to have a sibling, and that's a truth that should be allowed to stand. It's hard for the average parent who has put a new person in the world to tolerate even a scratch on them; they therefore fail to see through the eyes of the other person they adore, who has a very different perspective on the contents of the crib. Yet we need to allow them to hate so that they might one day love.

Therefore, when they tell us that the new baby is dreadful and stinks and is ugly, we have to bear with it. Remember how it would feel if it were a mistress or a lover. We wouldn't want to hear a lecture on how the lover was – in fact – beautiful. We wouldn't want our attention drawn to its adorable toes or winning ways of holding a spoon. We wouldn't want to overhear a conversation with a friend about how, the other day, it sang a pretty song and wore the most adorable trousers. We'd be very discreet about our love, not to be sly, but because we'd be sensitive to what was going on in our other loved one's mind. We would accept that we might have wanted two people to love but that this couldn't be an ideal scenario for either of our chosen ones. We wouldn't jolly them along; we would let them find their own way through the catastrophe.

When they were acting up, we wouldn't chide them for 'trying to get attention'. We would recognise their hunger and give them what they craved. We'd make sure we carved out regular time when we could be alone with them, like in the old days. We'd go on a few cosy trips, just the two of us. And when they got difficult out of jealousy, we wouldn't punish them for their sense of not being enough; we would give them the time and the love they were calling for through their hatred.

Then one day, when we'd given up expecting them to get on, we might knock at one of their doors and be told to go away. We'd hear them chatting like the best of friends and giggling a bit too. We'd find that they'd discovered a secret and illicit friend: their own sibling. We'd find that our focused, tolerant love for them had done its job: enabled them to see the point of one another.

10. Lessons in Play

The useful thing about children is that they don't let their imaginations get hampered by the more irritating or incidental aspects of reality. They will take one look at a sofa and see in it the basis for an ingenious spacecraft capable of travelling swiftly and comfortably to adjoining galaxies. An unprepossessing backyard will make the ideal premises for a new kind of restaurant offering fascinating combinations of food not yet developed in the ordinary restaurant sector. They will know how to size up a sibling and recognise a brave, disciplined and resolute national leader who will be able to lead her country out of its troubles and invent a new way of doing politics.

Children don't see a need to wait until every practical detail has been sorted out before beginning to imagine fresh schemes and develop original proposals. They know the gist of what has to be done and are keen to sketch out at speed the broad strokes of their plans. They have none of the normal adult respect for so-called sensible objections to every new idea, or obedience to the many reasons why something should not be tried and the status quo left morosely undisturbed.

Little children tend to be right in their hunch that the practical details can generally be sorted out with time, but that what one really needs at the outset is vision. Most impressive developments have been works of the imagination long before they were feats of engineering or politics, art or science. They were ideas that needed to be pictured with a fanciful, confident and unfrightened mind, one that would not curtail its freedoms by pointing out that something might cost too much, or that some members of the team might be unsettled by an innovation, or that there were government rules against that sort of thing.

Take flying as an example. On the one hand, powered flight was a practical breakthrough reliant on some steady work around wing shapes, petrol engines and landing gears. But there was arguably as much imagination in the plane as there was engineering; the plane had to be dreamt of before it could be designed. A lot of this imaginative work was carried

Albert Robida, *Leaving the Opera in the Year 2000*, 1902

out by pioneers of playful thought in the 19th century, the great age of technological daydreaming, when utopian big children imagined how one might fly between cities in miraculous heavier-than-air machines – and one day make it from Paris to New York in only a few hours.

These pioneers of technology also imagined email, submarines, cross-Channel tunnels, vacuum cleaners, mobile phones and digital education. It is a tribute to the scale of their ambitions that reality still has to catch up with their thoughts around jetpacks and winged firefighters.

Thanks to the aero-express, New York is only 1½ hours from London.
Price of a one-way trip: $1000 (disaster inclusive).

J. Xaudaro, *Concorde before Concorde*, 1920: '*Thanks to the aero-express, New York is only one and a half hours away from London. Price of the trip: 1,000 dollars.*'

Un Frotteur électrique

At School

Aerial Firemen

In the Year 2000, a series of French illustrations, 1899–1910

Children don't only have things to teach us around playfully imagining the future. They are also canny at coming up with imaginary friends. Reality can be very poor at providing us with the kinds of people we actually need in order to feel understood and comforted. What we long to hear and the sort of interactions we crave may not always be possible in the compromised conditions of a typical home. But this rarely holds children back. They will latch ingeniously onto a promising-looking thirty-centimetre piece of cloth and stuffing with button eyes and decide that this is the friend they always wished for and deserve: someone who can understand their sorrows, will have comforting things to say when they are confused, will want to have cups of tea with them in the night and will always, always be ready for a hug.

Later on, they may discover books and try out a similar move. These so called bookworms learn how to feel connected to a person who might have died in 1420 CE or 300 BCE and who tells them important things with a freshness and clarity no one in their vicinity can match. They take to carrying this friend around with them in a bag wherever they go, and don't mind if its corners get dirty or pages mottled. They stay up late with the 'friend' and might weep at a tenderness and understanding that seems so far from what they receive from their own acquaintances. A few of these children even go on to become writers, and one day confide to a page what it feels hard to express to others in person – a grown-up version of the move they might once have made in childhood, when their frayed bear patiently heard their upsets. Bookshops, the toy shops of big people, end as places where our disappointments with others can be mediated and redeemed, and friends not found in life can be secured through the grown-up game we soberly call 'literature'.

Tommy, the much-loved childhood companion of Mr J.H.B. Gowan, who continued to send him birthday cards even after he donated him to London's Victoria and Albert Museum.

The ideal position of play in life was first explored by the Ancient Greeks. Among all their gods, two mattered to them especially. The first was Apollo, god of reason and wisdom. He was concerned with patience, thoroughness, duty and logical thinking. He presided over aspects of government, commerce and what we would now call science. But there was another important god, a diametrically opposed figure whom the Greeks called Dionysus. He was concerned with the imagination, impatience, chaos, emotion, instinct – and play. The 'Dionysian' involved dreams, liberation and a relaxation of the strict rules of reason. Importantly, the Greeks did not think that any life could be complete without a combination of these two figures. Both Apollo and Dionysus had their claims on human lives, and each could breed dangerously unbalanced minds if they held undiluted sway.

When children have driven us to the edge of sanity with their games (along with the attendant shrieks, follies, destroyed sofas and gluey potions), we should keep in mind how much we, weary guardians of Apollo, remain in debt to all the young followers of Dionysus and their ever-present call to bend reality in the direction of our dreams.

11. Lessons in Confidence

A near-universal goal of parents is to try to imbue their children with confidence; to try to lend them the energy, self-belief and courage to eventually be able to act decisively in the world. With sufficient confidence, they will know how to go up to strangers and ask for help, push their interests forward at work, articulate their wishes to prospective partners and trust in their decency and right to exist.

But how to imbue this confidence remains a complex matter. The standard approach is to remind children of their qualities: whatever they may sometimes feel, we insist that they are clever. Whatever a few mean people might say, we tell them they are special. Whatever they may think in front of the mirror, we tell them they are beautiful. Whatever they sometimes fear, we say they are neither idiots nor fools. With such generous sentiments in their ears, children will – we trust – be able to confront their challenges without inadequacy. They will know that despite the difficulties, they are competent and deserving – and that the world should be grateful for their presence.

Although this sounds generous, exulting a child in this way may unwittingly generate whole new levels of doubt. The implication is that grounds for confidence are primarily derived from being clever, talented, beautiful and deserving. Yet by equating confidence with wondrousness, the child is being burdened with a forbidding picture of what is required for success. The bar is unconsciously being set in an elevated position; one is just being assured – slightly unbelievably – that one will clear it.

It might be better to push in a slightly different direction. Sensitive children are in danger of overestimating the adult world and thereby of throttling their talents and sense of initiative out of misfounded respect. It can seem to them as if teachers must know everything, so there is no need to think sceptically about most of what they teach. It can seem as if people at the top of important professions have been endowed with unusual degrees of intelligence, which makes their jobs impossible to get. And in their own peer group, it can look as though the popular and attractive people must have life securely worked out at every level, and could therefore have no need for a new friend or partner.

In this context, it may help a young person to be given access to some apparently dark but in the end liberating truths about the adult world. Despite certain appearances, and a lot of puffery and decorum, human beings are not on the whole an especially clever, competent, knowledgeable or respectable species. Indeed, as a rule, they are properly idiotic and rather damnable. The path to confidence is not to build up a child; it is to knock down society as a whole.

To appease a child's terror that they might be stupid, rather than telling them that they are brilliant, one should let them know a far more cheering and believable idea: that they have foolish sides, but so has everyone else. They are definitely sometimes idiots, but so is the headmistress, the geography teacher, the president, the finance minister, the Nobel Prize winner, the great novelist, the zoologist, the movie star and all parents who have ever lived. There is no other option for a human being. We are a planet of seven billion idiots. We walk into doors, get things wrong, proffer moronic ideas, spill things down our fronts, forget our own names and ruin our lives – and these aren't exceptions; they are the general rule. A worry that one might be a bit stupid doesn't therefore mark one as special or specially damned; it makes one more like every other human in history. It certainly isn't an argument for not trying to join a team or asking someone on a date, for refusing to apply to a particular university or imagine oneself in a given career.

We should remind children that they know themselves from the inside, but can know others only from the outside – that is, via what these others choose to mention, which results in an unhelpfully limited and edited picture of normality. While they will be aware of every detail of their own inadequacies, there will be little evidence of the inadequacies of others. We should stress to children that beneath serious and self-assured facades, all peers and impressive grown-ups are sunk in doubt, fear and regret. Wishing to make his readers more confident, the 16th-century philosopher Montaigne wrote: 'Kings and philosophers shit and so do ladies.' Shitting was here intended as a representative term, symbolic of all the lower, more embarrassing and weaker dimensions we know about in ourselves but have a hard time remembering exist in others. Montaigne might have added that these august people also tend to worry, feel ugly and say daft things. And not only them, but also presidents, heads of law firms, top footballers and serious-looking teachers.

There is a kind of child who won't dare to act, thinking that one mistake will place them forever in the camp of the contemptible. One should reassure them that being a fool is not a personal risk; it is a common and inviolable rule. If they took action and ended up doing one more silly thing, it wouldn't be special grounds for shame; it would merely be confirming what they had understood from the start: that we are all, often in rather endearing ways, error-prone beings. The path to confidence is not to banish fears that one might be silly; it is to not let knowledge of one's silliness become grounds for a refusal to act. The task is not to tell children that they are amazing; it is to model for them how one might live a decent, self-accepting, humour-filled and confident life knowing one is very imperfect – but, fortunately, so is everyone else.

12. Lessons in Relationships

A central part of any parent's responsibility is to prepare children for the challenges of adulthood: getting a job, managing finances, writing timely thank you letters, brushing hair, hanging up wet coats … What is less frequently mentioned is that if this training is to be adequate to the real requirements of adulthood, then it should also include one subject that more than any other determines a person's chances of leading a successful life: the ability to form and maintain intimate relationships.

This topic can be excruciating to discuss head on within a family, but the good news is that no formal instruction is truly necessary here. One won't have to deliver classes on how to invite someone on a date or how to ask a partner for more time alone. Yet the lack of a need for direct education doesn't absolve parents of all responsibility; it just shifts it into the indirect realm.

Teaching about relationships goes on continually within families, without warning, in diverse and sometimes counter-intuitive ways. As parents, we might be covering essential parts of the relationship curriculum without realising it while setting up a treehouse or having a race in the corridor, breaking up a fight between siblings or discussing who should wash up. Far more than defined lessons, these borderless 'classroom' hours in the home are when children will actually learn – or fail to learn – the components of satisfactory adult relationships.

These disguised emotional learning modules might include some of the following topics:

Integration

In trying to understand relationships, the pioneering mid-20th-century Viennese psychoanalyst Melanie Klein drew attention to a feeling that can unfold in the minds of babies during feeding sessions with their mothers. When feeding goes well, the baby is blissfully content and sees their mother as very 'good'. But if, for whatever reason, the feeding process is difficult, the baby can't grasp that it is dealing with the same person it liked a lot only a few hours or minutes ago. So it splits off from the actual mother a second 'bad' version – whom it deems to be a separate, hateful individual, responsible for deliberately frustrating its wishes – and, in the process, protects the image of the good mother in its mind. Gradually, if things go well, there follows a long and difficult process by which the child 'integrates' these two different people and comes to grasp that there is no ideal, 'perfect' mother, but nor is there a terrible and awful one either; there is just one person who is usually lovely but can also be cross, busy, tired, mistaken or interested in other people.

Parents can help their children in the task of integration by presenting a holistic image of themselves, neither sentimentally and deceitfully sweet nor unfairly aggressive or sadistic. Ideally, the child will realise that their parent can be both fundamentally decent and in a bad mood right now, or in essence well intentioned but annoying about homework this evening. Children who have lived with a less rounded parent (in either starkly negative or unrealistically positive directions) will find integration harder. They may develop tendencies to fall deeply in love with people whom they insist on idealising, but they may suddenly and violently turn against them the moment they discover a detail that disturbs or frustrates them.

They may find it hard to accept that the same person might be very nice and good in some ways and strikingly disappointing in others. The bad version can appear to destroy the good one, though these are really just different and connected aspects of one complex person. To help a child cope with their conflicts between hope and reality, parents might combine love with a free admission of all that is imperfect in themselves. That way, their child will be gently reminded that no one we love will ever satisfy us completely, but they aren't worth hating on that score. Children will be able to move from the hopeful naïvety and rage of the splitting phase to the mature wisdom of the integrative one. They will know that they can end up with a partner who, in their blend of qualities and frailties, is eminently 'good enough'.

Being loved

How much a parent of the gender we are drawn to finds us loveable is, to a humbling degree, likely to influence how acceptable we end up feeling about ourselves. The memory of having been cherished and deemed interesting by a parent guides the way we evaluate the face staring back at us in the mirror in adulthood or moulds how we imagine strangers might respond to our invitations for dinner. Those who failed to interest their parents may struggle to believe that anyone will ever notice them.

They may be driven either to sabotage relationships in their early stages in order to return to a solitude that feels more deserved and safe, or to keep seducing new people in order to prove to themselves that they have an appeal of which they are never truly convinced (manic promiscuity having little to do with enjoying sex, and a lot to do with feeling wretched). But equal damage can be done by parents who lend a child an eerie impression that they play too great a role in their emotional lives and are the subject of excessive admiration and interest, leaving the child with a guilty sense that they might be being disloyal to a parent if they eventually built a secure relationship with someone else, or that they are powerless to stand up to those who disregard their boundaries.

The emotionally healthy parent implies that their child is an extremely valuable person, but for somebody else, many years from now, to get together with – and that their relationship with them, though joyful, does not compensate them for gaps in their own emotional life.

Communication

Young children are typically equipped with a charming but troublesome sense that those around them may be able to understand them without them needing to speak. This, after all, tends to be their first experience of how relationships work, when in their youngest days a parent seemed magically to intuit that milk was required or that a bath would be handy. From this a child may evolve an impression that those who truly love them will and must be able to know wordlessly what is in their minds – and by implication, that those who guess wrongly are unloving and perhaps even evil. The tuned-in parent will learn how to catch this presumption in its early stages. With kindness and humour, they will force the child to articulate needs that they might otherwise have left unsaid and keep pointing out that unless the child speaks, another person (even a very lovely other person) cannot possibly know what they want or are going through. The parent will lavish praise on any stumbling attempts at detailed communication, and be correspondingly unimpressed by sulks – those peculiar phenomena in which one person blames another for not understanding them, even though they have not deigned to share what the problem might be. A sound childhood awakens us to the tedious responsibility to explain.

The body

A capacity to have successful adult relationships will depend to a significant degree on being comfortable with one's own body – in particular with many of the so-called 'lower' appetites and desires that the body involves us in, which can contrast markedly with the demands of dignified adult life. It is not the task of a parent to discuss the intimate side of their progeny's lives, but to a surprising extent, ease in this area is the consequence of having had benevolent experiences of a secretly related kind in the early years. It is in the remit of parents to give young children a natural and forgiving relationship with their own sensory consciences, forged over a range of proxy issues.

For example, a parent may send out a message that it doesn't matter that the child got muddy in the playground or that their boot fell into a smelly pond; they might make some mud pies along with the child and encourage them to enjoy the oozing sensation of earth and water squeezing out of their palms. They might laugh sweetly at a child's farts or smile indulgently at its occasionally bawdy delight in scooping vast amounts of strawberry jam onto some toast at breakfast. The parent might imply that it's OK to take delight in one's own voice and sometimes let out a succession of joyful piercing rhythmic screams from the top of the stairs, or to indulge in an exuberant pillow fight with a sibling. Far more than any ungainly lecture on relationships, this will be enough to ensure that a child knows that its body can be a source of pleasure and creativity rather than guilt and shame.

Repetition

It has been the work of a century of psychotherapy to introduce humanity to a troubling idea: that the way we choose our partners in our adult lives has a lot to do with our relationships with our parents in our early years. This is troubling because we like to feel that we will be able to make our own choices rather than following a script written for us by other people, and because this repetition of childhood patterns often suggests that we will be recreating relationships of sorrow rather than of joy.

The good enough parent accepts that the psychotherapeutic story may, however difficult it sounds, be true – but they will try to ensure that it need not be a disaster, that following a template set in childhood does not have to involve offspring in patterns of suffering. These parents will do everything they can to turn the therapeutic prophecy that one might unknowingly marry one's mother or father from the tragedy it is generally assumed to be into a more bearable and even heart-warming possibility.

13. Lessons in Issues

For much of the modern era, the story of becoming an adult has been told to us as one of psychological liberation: as they grow up, people will notice how many of their difficulties, especially around love and work, can be traced back to inadequacies in their childhoods. They will realise, for example, how much their low self-esteem owes to their relationship with a withholding mother, or how much of their timidity at work can be traced back to an over-anxious father. Slowly people will develop their full potential by reflecting on what happened in their childhood and by untangling the past with the help of friends, diaries and, most importantly, kind and well-trained psychotherapists.

This story, though powerful, tends to miss out on a crucial stage: what happens when these victims of childhood become parents themselves. Relatively little is said about what these former children might do when they take on the mantle of parenthood in turn. How might they fare with the momentous responsibilities that their parents mishandled? How might they ensure that their own children do not have to suffer from another cycle of psychological mishap? How might they avoid passing on their 'issues'?

It is helpful to be categorical and unsentimental on this score: there is no option not to pass on some of one's issues; there is no way of parenting that does not inflict some form of psychological damage on children. The most psychotherapised person in the world will not be able to avoid generating neuroses; there is no such thing as a blameless parent. Above the door of the nursery, the most emotionally mature parent should still hang a sign: 'I love you – but I will give you issues.'

Once this idea is established, the priorities can shift. It is no longer a matter of trying to avoid damage altogether, but of doing one's best to mitigate it. The parent should appreciate that they are – as we all are – a bit damaged and should know a bit more about how and why. They should be able to answer the question: *how are you mad?*

Nothing insulting or unusual should be read into this enquiry; it is a precondition of being human that we are mad in some way. However, the way our minds work can shield us from an awareness of quite how and in what areas we might be mad – information that is crucial to softening the damage. In order to kick-start our self-knowledge, we might undertake a small exercise to try to reveal for ourselves some of the many ways in which we are disturbed and likely to mess up the lives of those we adore beyond measure.

Possible Parental Issues		
Despite my great love for my child(ren), I might make the following mistakes because of my issues ...	**Yes**	**No**
• I might be so traumatised by harshness and arbitrary commands in my childhood that I might be unable to set boundaries or say 'no' when I should.		
• I might alternate between relaxedness and sudden fury, which could bewilder a sensitive child.		
• I might be unable to prevent the enormous anxiety that I feel at work from spilling over into family life.		

• Because of my introverted nature, I might be unable to participate as regularly and intensely in family activities as I would like to.		
• Because of certain sexual compulsions, I might be unable to play the role of the reliable family man or woman.		
• Because of deficiencies in my current relationship, I might over-invest in my child and thereby prevent them from developing healthily.		
• Because of my fragilities, I might lead a child to need to take care of me emotionally in a way that could prompt them to take on the mantle of adulthood prematurely.		
• Because of my envy and resentment at the way I've been treated in life, I might give my child a sense that the world is an unwelcoming place that they should fear.		
• I might have difficulty with a particular gender of child because of my experiences with that sex.		
• I might be drawn to have a favourite child and play one off against the other.		
• I might be appalled by a child's vulnerability and tell them, far too young, to grow up and stop whining.		

• I might feel jealous of my child's success.		
• I won't be able to stay sane around mess and noise.		
• I might take it personally if my child is not sufficiently impressive at school.		

This is only a start; there could be much else to discover. The crucial point is to know that one has a large number of issues and that their effect is likely to be powerful.

The next step is to share the information in the least dramatic way possible with one's children as soon as they are in a position to understand. It is a huge drawback for a child if their parent is over-interested in suggesting that they are totally sane and psychologically competent. In the interests of maintaining troop morale, many parents will feel under pressure to put on a 'good show', especially in the early years, framing themselves as always sane, inevitably calm, perpetually smiley and invariably on top of things. But in order properly to assist children with their mental well-being, it would be far more helpful if these parents could shake off their pride and gently hint at how they are in fact a bit strange. It is an enormous privilege to receive advance knowledge of one's parent's neuroses from the parent themselves, especially if the information is imparted with self-deprecating humour in an unalarming manner. Subsequently, this child won't have to spend a few decades on the therapist's couch trying to figure out whether and how their parent was disturbed. The issues will have been freely shared a long time before.

Parents often like to explain – and children to hear about – where a family originated: where Granddad was born, who Granny married the first time, what Dad did after finishing school and so on. To these external movements, one might think of adding a psychological layer, explaining the patterns of emotional inheritance. A child might then be able to give a friend in the playground or an interested adult a handy summary of the issues their parents were afflicted by:

Mummy's father was quite depressed and that means she's found it hard to trust men, but eventually Daddy came along and got her to relax, but she's still quite independent-minded and likes to be alone for ages – and that leads them to conflicts. Daddy had a distant mother and a judgemental father (maybe that's why he picked Mum!). It makes him pretty anxious and on a bad day prone to shouting. It also makes him a bit fussy about me and cloying and always hovering around, like he wants everything to go right for me to compensate for what went badly for him. That's also probably why I tell him to go away a lot, quite fiercely.

The greatest available form of sanity isn't to lack issues; it is to be willing to understand and admit to them. The more one knows them, the less likely one is to have to play them out. It is a huge source of relief to children to grow up in a family where issues are discussed with as little embarrassment as a sore back or a headache; it should be as customary to hear an adult complaining about their anxiety as their bad toe, or about their low self-esteem as their worries about politics. Far from creating a child who will be fussy or susceptible, one will be modelling how to maintain a self-aware, relaxed, undefensive relationship to psychological difficulties. Being able to share issues belongs to a slow pattern of progress whereby humans have learnt to come to terms with their vulnerability and accept themselves as only intermittently rational; our strength lies in being able to accept our own fragility.

14. Lessons in Crying

One of the wisest things about young children is that they have no shame or compunction about bursting into tears, perhaps because they have a more accurate and less pride-filled sense of their place in the world. They know they are small beings in a hostile and unpredictable realm, that they can't control much of what is happening around them, that their powers of understanding are limited and that there is a great deal to feel distressed, melancholy and confused about. Why not then, on a fairly regular basis, sometimes for only a few moments at a time, collapse into some highly salutary sobs at the sheer scale of the sorrow of being alive?

Unfortunately, such wisdom tends to get lost as we age. We get taught to avoid being that most apparently repugnant (and yet in fact deeply philosophical) of creatures: the cry-baby. We start to associate maturity with a suggestion of invulnerability and competence. We imagine it might be sensible to imply that we are unfailingly strong and in command.

But this is reckless. Realising one can no longer cope is an integral part of true competence; we should let young children be our teachers (and remind adolescents of this wisdom in turn). We are in our essence, and should always strive to remain, cry-babies – that is, people who intimately remember their susceptibility to hurt and grief. Moments of losing courage belong to a brave life.

We labour under the misapprehension that the only thing that could justify tears would be one clear and unambiguous catastrophe. But that is to forget how many minuscule elements go wrong every hour, how much supposedly 'small things' can impact us and how heavy they may end up feeling.

When the impulse to cry strikes us, we should be grown-up enough to consider ceding to it as we knew how to in the sagacity of our fourth or fifth years. We might repair to a quiet room, put the duvet over our heads and give way to unrestrained torrents at the horribleness of it all. We easily forget how much energy we normally have to expend fending off despair; now at last we can properly allow despondency to have its way. No thought should be too dark any more: we are obviously no good. Everyone is evidently mean. It's naturally far too much. Our life is – undoubtedly – meaningless and ruined. If the session is to work, we need to touch the very bottom and make ourselves at home there.

Then, if we have properly done our work, at some point we'll begin to cheer up again. We'll remember that it would be pleasant to have a hot bath, that we have a few good friends on the planet and an interesting book still to read – and we'll know that the worst of the storm is over.

Despite our adult powers of reasoning, the needs of childhood constantly thrum within us. We are never far from craving to be held and reassured, as we might have been decades ago by a sympathetic adult, most likely a parent, who made us feel physically protected, kissed our forehead, looked at us with benevolence and tenderness and perhaps said not much other than, very quietly, 'Of course.' To be in need of Mummy (as it were) is to risk ridicule, especially when we are a couple of metres tall and in a position of responsibility.

Yet to understand and accept one's younger longings belongs to the essence of genuine adulthood – and parenthood. There is no maturity without an adequate negotiation with the infantile, and no such thing as a proper grown-up who does not frequently yearn to be comforted like a toddler.

With all this in mind, we should take care not to toughen up our children too much. We should never call them cry-babies; we should give them permission to be vulnerable. In sensible households, we should all – however old we are – have signs, a bit like those in hotels, that we can hang on our doors and announce to passers-by that we are spending a few minutes inside doing something essential to our humanity and inherently connected to our capacity be content: sobbing for a little while like a lost small child.

15. Lessons in Discipline

One of the harder tasks facing parents is how to discipline: the imperative to declare in a certain voice that the moment to stop eating ice cream is now; that though it's been fun jumping on the sofa, this is going to be the last softly voiced request to go upstairs; that obviously no one is getting any sort of phone – new or second-hand – if homework is not completed.

Part of what makes discipline hard is that, in response to our 'no', we will have to hear that we have ruined someone's life, that we are the worst person in the world and that we will never, ever be forgiven – a paradoxical position when the red-faced, tear-stained person screaming this also happens to be the creature we most adore on the planet and for whom we would lay down our lives.

Discipline may be universally challenging, but its exigencies can be felt and studied with particular clarity in a subset of parents beset by one of the most poignant of psychological afflictions: people-pleasing. On the face of it, being someone who pleases people sounds like a good idea. But it is a pattern of behaviour riddled with unintended difficulty, as much for the perpetrator as for their audience. The people-pleaser is someone (who might at times be us) who feels they have no option but to mould themselves to the expectations of others. At work, they will strive to accommodate the demands of all those around them; in social life, they will smile with pointed grace at the jokes and anecdotes of wearying acquaintances. In their relationships, they will be unable to lodge a complaint against a casually selfish partner. And as parents, it will be close to impossible for them to exit a toy shop or a bakery without buying something they shouldn't.

The origins of people-pleasing tend to lie far back in childhood – in a painful encounter with discipline. People-pleasers' pasts almost invariably involved an experience of being around caregivers who demanded an elevated degree of submission. Perhaps a father or mother flew into volcanic rage at any sign of disagreement. To present an opposing political idea, to suggest that they wanted something different to eat, to be frank about tiredness or anxiety was to be threatened with annihilation. There was no possibility of causing a fuss or stamping one's feet or insisting on another ice cream. To survive, the child needed to tread on eggshells and be acutely responsive to whatever was expected of them. The question of what they might really want or think became secondary to the greater priority of moulding themselves to the desires of those on whom their lives depended at that time. They pleased and smiled out of a longing not to set off another ugly row, to keep a terrifyingly irate person calm or to avoid adding a further burden to what seemed like already difficult and sad lives.

As people-pleasers approached parenthood, they may have indulged in a double fantasy; first, that they would be able to avoid everything connected to the sort of childhood they had. They wouldn't need to shout or deny; they wouldn't have to tyrannise or insist on rules. Made miserable by harshness, they were hopeful that they could run a household exclusively on gentleness.

Secondly, and relatedly, they may have imagined that their child's demands would be fundamentally reasonable. They pictured a child who was wise, by nature polite, modest and capable of innate self-command. They would have been guided in this by remembering how apparently reasonable they had been, how uninclined they had been to be difficult and wilful – though they would perhaps have forgotten that they had been meek not so much out of choice as out of cowed necessity. It was not as if they hadn't wanted, at some level, to have a powerful tantrum in the zoo or go wild in the toy shop; it's that they would have been vaporised if they had even dared to think of it.

How surprising then for the people-pleasing parent to encounter the likely reality of their own child, an often-adorable human with some perplexing characteristics nevertheless: an inclination to refuse certain politely worded requests and to shout and scream instead. The parent's fantasies might have been of a quiet relationship marked by mutual respect; the reality might be a series of intense conflicts.

The priority for the people-pleasing parent is not so much to learn how to discipline (that might come with time) as to grasp *why they might need to do so*. They need to tell themselves the right sort of story about why they have ended up having to expend so much effort saying 'no'. The central move is to keep two facts of psychology in mind: that humans are not built in such a way as directly to recognise their own best long-term interests; and that their powers of reasoning are constantly assaulted by the influence of powerful and highly questionable appetites and desires.

A child may speak with certainty about aspirations for things that, if they were to receive them, would run wholly counter to their benefit – or just kill them. They might insist to the last and yet be wrong. For a time at least (a decade or more), the parent is likely to understand the child's interests far better than the child themselves – a position of extreme epistemological superiority of which the people-pleasing parent will instinctively be wary. It is not in their nature to insist on their own predominant wisdom. And yet, faced with their furious toddler shouting that they want to pull the dog's tail or eat a handful of moss, they might – almost for the first time – discover that they really do have a claim on the nature of reality that exceeds another's. Whatever their instinctive hatred of authority, they might really know better what happens when you put your fingers in the socket or spend seven hours in a row online. Parental love will – at last – give them the courage to defend their hitherto wavering convictions. Out of love, they will drop their exhausting concern with politeness and accommodation. Out of love they will strap their beloved to their car seat and let out a loud and definitive 'no'.

Through the business of parenting, the people-pleaser will have to become that very surprising thing: a sensible, kindly, generous but firm *people-frustrater*. In order to honour their love for someone, they will learn that they need, for a time at least, to make their child deeply unhappy. They will see that there is no possibility of safeguarding a child and going along with all of the child's proposals. They will sometimes have to prevent them from getting what they want in order to provide them with what they need.

In the process, the people-pleasing parent may have to rethink their own past. They will have to recognise that their sceptical attitudes to authority may have been shaped by a specific set of irate caregivers, but that, in life more broadly, it might be possible to be authoritative *and* kind, certain *and* polite, unyielding *and* sympathetic. Combinations of emotions unknown in their own past will emerge. They will develop a feel for a third way, an assertive kindness somewhere between passive acceptance on the one hand and bullying on the other.

The people-pleasing parent may concurrently realise that it is reassuring for a child to feel that they are being denied certain of their wishes. It's no fun for a small person to have to bear a sense that they are totally in charge. An impression of omnipotence is terrifying for an undeveloped human, because it is synonymous with being alone and essentially uncared for. If no one can control them, then – logically – no one has the strength to look after them. If no one bothers to say 'no', then no one minds what will happen to them. Despite the child's fury and cocksure declarations, they understand – outside the limited sphere of the toy shop or the bedtime routine – that they need someone strong enough to frustrate them. They have a sufficiently instinctive grasp on their own immaturity to appreciate the love that lies behind discipline. They have enough of a nascent adult mind to know that they are a child.

To comfort the people-pleasing parent for the considerable distress of having had to raise their voice, it may help to offer them congratulations for having a child who dares to stand up to them. What an achievement of love it is to bring up someone who is secure enough to be a bit repulsive at points – and is sufficiently at ease to be able to discharge their full reserves of hatred on a parent. In turn, what a testament to parental security to know how to stand witness to a volcanic eruption of rage and to be neither crushed by it nor provoked to fury. Their child isn't 'difficult' or 'spoilt'; it's properly alive, and so naturally wants to try out a few wild things (as they should themselves have done at that age, had conditions been more benevolent). Yet it also wants to be told, without any embarrassment, that it can't have what it wants and has to go to bed right now.

Along the way, the people-pleaser may learn something else that their past didn't equip them with: the art of disappointing someone well. Slowly they will find the confidence to be deft around the difficult messages that have to be imparted. As a child they couldn't nuance their messages. They didn't know how to craft their raw pain and needs into convincing explanations; all they saw their parents do was scream and order. But now it is open to them to be resolute in their views – but sometimes rather genial as well. They may say 'no' while indicating that they feel a lot of goodwill; they can say their sweet little one is wrong without implying that they are an idiot. *They can be pleasant without being people-pleasers.*

One way to conceive of the task of being a parent is that it is essentially concerned with having to break bad news. The job is to let a child down, systematically and steadily, as to the nature of reality; to move them from a belief in their own boundlessness and unlimited authority and the capacity of the world to honour their every desire, to the point where they can accept a range of limitations and appalling compromises, including the fact that they are going to die. To be a good parent is to be a kindly shepherd to the tragic facts of existence.

The hopeful temptation for the child when its wishes are being denied is to imagine that it has been served up an unusually stupid and wrong-headed example of an adult – and that, with sufficient luck, when this adult dies or can be pushed aside, greater satisfaction will prevail. But one must insist on a far more painful and sober truth: that the disappointment of which one happens to be the instigator is not some local and avoidable phenomenon; it belongs to the bitterness of life itself. The child is meeting sadness and misery at the hands of a parent, but it is not the fault of the parent. They may be blaming us, but we might add (with great kindness and considerable melancholy in our voice) that they should really direct their ire at a more fitting target: a silent and indifferent universe.

Nevertheless, we should be as sweet as possible in as many areas as possible so that when we finally have to say 'no', the child will trust that we are not simply a tyrant, and that perhaps, just perhaps, there may be some truth lurking behind our maddeningly pessimistic dictates. One might hint at how many compromises and strictures there are in our own lives: even though we are allowed to drive a car and stay up late, in a hundred other matters we too are hemmed in and might like to live differently, if only we were allowed to. We should give our children an early, gentle taste of how much unhappiness and resignation all halfway decent lives exact.

16. Lessons in Resilience

Children spend a lot of time worrying: that there is a monster under the bed; that a gigantic cat might take them away in the night; that a flood might sweep away their home. When they seek comfort in the early hours from the terrors of their dreams, they tell us of having imagined being buried alive, being chased by dogs down into underground car parks or having their legs chewed off by a herd of one-eyed zebras.

To appease their worries, we take them in our arms and tell them that it will all be OK, that there is nothing to be concerned about, that they are safe and that the world will do them none of the harm they dread. Schools send out the same message: humans have it under control; teachers know the way (they just need to be listened to); there is no need for panic. The doctors are equally reassuring and have fascinating stethoscopes too; it's just a scrape, it will heal up in a few days, a bit of cream and it will be gone. And bedtime stories do their best to tie things up neatly: the kangaroo and its mum lived happily ever after; the girl recovered the family fortune; the owl made it back to its nest; the moon rediscovered its place in the sky. It was, and always will be, fine in the end. It's time for bed now. No, we can't have another one. Night night, soldier.

We think, by following a path of optimism, that we are making our child resilient and preparing them for a sometimes rough world. We are not always wrong, but might there be occasional space for a darker but equally and perversely more calming approach? What if we began to picture what might happen if the owl got lost and the girl didn't find the money? What if we think about what it would be like if a few things did go wrong and a bit of cream didn't put it right? We are so scared of scaring children, might we be making them more afraid by shielding them from what is properly daunting?

For the Stoic philosophers of Ancient Rome, the way to find calm was not to insist that bad things don't happen. They can and do happen all the time – maybe not exactly in the way that small children imagine them, but often pretty close. There are famines and plagues, fires and wars. There are some dangerous animals and some horrible people. There are horrific diseases and there is death. But crucially, the Stoics insisted, although these things are possible, they can be endured to a far greater extent than we're inclined to think. They can be thought through and mastered by our minds. We must not leave them as unexplored worries and shove them to the back of consciousness; that is to give them victory and allow them to unsettle us perpetually. Even our own death can be measured up to and the spectre confronted. There aren't always happy endings; it's nothing like what children's stories imply, but maybe there can be a route through nevertheless, if we look at what our options are in the midst of calamity.

'To find calm,' wrote the philosopher Seneca, 'imagine not what will probably happen, but what can happen.' In other words, picture the worst, push your worries to their limits and see what it would be like; it might not be pretty, but it might be OK in its way. The Stoics advised running through the most awful scenarios – disgrace, poverty, the loss of a limb or two, an epidemic – and trying to analyse their terrors head on. The route to inner strength is not to run away from anxiety; it is to switch on the light in the room of fear and see what the contents really are. If there were a flood, how could we cope? If there were a plague, how might we manage? If we got a diagnosis, what might we do next?

The most Stoic story in the history of children's literature was written and illustrated by the German-born British writer Judith Kerr and first published in 1968. *The Tiger Who Came to Tea* tells the story of a little girl called Sophie who is having tea with her mother when there is a ring at the door. It is – as it can sometimes be in life – a tiger. A natural response would be to panic. It might be normal to scream. It would be extremely understandable if one lost all will to live. But Sophie's mother appears to have read Seneca and perhaps Marcus Aurelius too and takes the new visitor in her stride. It's not an ideal outcome, but it's not grounds for consternation either. Stuff happens – and the mother might have expected something like this. So she sets about trying to appease the tiger's hunger.

She gives him all the food they have and stands back. He ransacks the cupboards; he swallows everything around; he bashes the kitchen about; he even empties the taps of their last drops of water. And then he goes away. When Sophie's father comes home from work, he's rather dismayed that there's no food left, but the

Judith Kerr, *The Tiger Who Came to Tea*, 1968

parents decide that this might be a great occasion to go out for a meal, so they head off and have something delicious in a nearby café. The next day, Sophie and her mother restock the house. They find a big tin of tiger food and buy it 'just in case'. But in fact, the tiger doesn't return. It may have been terrifying, but it was a one-off visit. Life goes on. Tigers come for tea – and then they move on.

The Stoics would have called *The Tiger Who Came to Tea* a premeditation, or an exploration of a difficult scenario designed to show us that it can happen but that it can also be borne. We do our children an injustice when we guess that they can only bear happiness. Like all humans, they are wired for catastrophe. The most loving and realistic thing is not to pretend that fearsome events don't befall us; they may, and they can destroy what we value along the way. The key move when we are scared is to stay with our fears long enough to probe what the dreadful things can really do to us and analyse matters to the point where we can perceive that we could endure what appeared disastrous from afar. It's to know that tigers will come and that, after some trouble and considerable damage, they tend to go away again.

17. Lessons in Manners

One of the first, and most boring, lessons children receive is on the importance of being 'kind' (as adults put it). It is because of this peculiar-seeming imperative that a parent will remind a child up to fifteen times in a single week to send Granny a thank you letter for the horrible hat she knitted them. Or that they have to add a 'please' every time they ask for almost anything, even a paper napkin, from anyone. This leaves children in little doubt: kindness is both important and entirely stupid.

As children grow up, they get better at the superficial mechanics of kindness, but not necessarily better at understanding why kindness should matter. The subject remains under some of the same strict or sentimental cloud beneath which it was first introduced to them as toddlers. They just succumb to its dictates more readily and are a little swifter with the cards.

The true reason why politeness matters boils down to a thought that parents may resist sharing with their children for a long time: that adults are alarmingly, and almost limitlessly, sensitive. They are unconvinced of their own value, their right to exist, their legitimacy, their claims on love, their decency and their capacity to interest anyone in their pains and in their ultimate fates. They need kindness so desperately, even its tiniest increments (a door held open, a compliment on a biscuit, a birthday remembered), not because they are attached to decorum for the sake of it, but because they are permanently teetering over a precipice of despair and self-loathing. The impression of grown-up self-assurance is a sham; inside, just beneath a layer of competence, they are terrified and lost, unsure and unreassured – and ready to cling to any sign, however small, that they deserve to continue.

It is understandable if adults were to try to hide this kind of susceptibility from their children (and themselves), or forget to mention it, and to present the need for kindness as flowing from some abstract requirement for obedience. What few parents dare to tell their children is that if Granny doesn't get the card, she might wake up in the early hours – a few weeks from now – and wonder whether anything she ever does is really worth it, whether she has wasted her whole life and whether this little rejection isn't part of a long-standing pattern of things never working out for her. It might feel too much to tell a child, with their untarnished hopes for the future, but we truly are creatures who will worry about an off-hand remark, and who may fall into self-loathing because someone jostled us in a shop or didn't say thank you for a pencil. What we call being polite is a way of lending others some small change in the emotional currency of hope and courage upon which we depend for our survival.

Children become invested in being kind when they are helped to realise the power they possess in a surprising number of situations to rescue another human from self-contempt. They start to be kind too when they realise how much they need others to be kind to *them*. It isn't an obvious thought. They may imagine that they don't mind how others behave, because people around them have generally been so kind; it is hard to notice the presence of what one has never been without.

Children may feel that they aren't going to allow themselves to be wounded so easily, adopting some of the pseudo-bravery of a 6-year-old who leaves the house on a wintry day without its overcoat, despite the entreaties of its parents. But gradually, they may come to know their own hearts slightly better, and feel their own pains more sincerely, and therefore realise that they are at the mercy of those with whom they interact. They may find themselves sad and listless at the end of a day at school; rather than distracting themselves with the internet or taking their frustration out on the dog, they may register that they are feeling defeated because a person at school didn't invite them to join in a game or laughed a bit too loudly at someone else's joke. Or they might register that they are really upset that someone they liked didn't mention they'd been shopping with a rival.

When they in turn have a child, they may find themselves insisting that they write a letter quickly, though they should add – if they know themselves well enough – something that might just get the letter written with a bit more feeling: that if Granny doesn't hear from them, she might get sad, she might start to worry about herself, she might wonder if she wasn't good at being a granny ...

We don't ultimately prompt anyone to grow kind by making them think about manners. We do so by helping them to think about the fear and self-hatred that others can lapse into without the comforts of kindness. In order to generate thoughtful children, parents shouldn't insist on the rules of propriety without a commentary. They should help their children by opening their eyes to an implausible thought about human nature: the extent of the insecurity felt by other people (even very big ones) and their corresponding susceptibility to shame and loneliness, their longing for reassurance and their craving for any sign (however small, even the size of a card with a pretty hand-drawn bird on the front) of their right to exist.

18. Lessons in Adolescence

One of the more calming thoughts for all parents is the knowledge that there is such a thing as normality for a given age.

For example, when one is 13, it is normal to hate one's parents, to wear unusual clothes, to spend all one's time in one's room, to play computer games incessantly, to speak in a monotone, to feel wholly misunderstood and to dismiss every other family member as an idiot. This isn't madness, as it would be in an adult; it's called being 13. It would be almost alarming if it were any other way.

Like all teenagers, 13-year-olds are miserable. Being grumpy is never beautiful to behold, but if there is any period of life in which the mood can be justified and in certain ways deemed important, it is in the span between 13 and 20. It is hard to imagine going on to have a successful or even somewhat contented next six decades if one has not been the beneficiary of a good deal of agonising introspection, grunting, weeping and intense dislocation in this period.

At the root of adolescent sorrow and rage is the recognition that life is harder, more absurd and less fulfilling than one could ever have suspected, or had been led to suppose by kindly representatives of the adult world. The sentimental protection of childhood falls away, and, to one's great anger, a range of horrible but profoundly important realisations come into view.

For a start, one recognises that no one understands who one really is. That isn't entirely true, but the more complicated any human being is, the less likely they are to be easily and immediately understood. Therefore, as a child develops into an adult, the chances of those around them exactly sympathising with and swiftly grasping their inner condition necessarily decrease sharply.

The first response of the teenager is to think themselves uniquely cursed. But the better eventual insight is that true connection with another person is astonishingly rare. This leads one to a number of important moves.

Firstly, to a heightened and more appropriate sense of gratitude towards anyone who does understand. Secondly, to greater efforts to make oneself understood. The sullen grunts of early adolescence may give way to the eloquence of the poetry, diaries and songs of later teenagehood. Some of the most beautiful pieces of communication humanity has ever produced have been the work of young people who couldn't find anyone they could talk to.

Lastly, the sense that one is different from other people, though it may be problematic at the time, represents a critical moment when a new generation starts to probe at and improve upon the existing order. To be 16 and find everything perfect as it is would be a terrifying and sterile conclusion. A refusal to accept the folly, error and evil of the world is a precondition of achievement. There really seems no alternative but to be miserable in mid-adolescence if one is to stand any chance of making a go of the rest of one's life.

Another key realisation of adolescence is that one hates one's parents. It is truly an enormous tribute to the love of parents if their teenage children turn around and tell them at the top of their voice that they loathe them. It isn't a sign that something has gone wrong; it's evidence that the child knows they are loved. The really worrying teenagers aren't those who misbehave around their parents and take out their random misery upon them; it's those who are so worried about not being loved that they can't afford to put a foot wrong.

To develop proper trust in other human beings, it can be important to be able to test a few examples, to tell them the worst things one can think of and then watch them stick around and forgive one. You have to have a few goes at breaking love to believe it can be solid.

Of course, parents are annoying in many ways. But that too is an important realisation. We would never leave home and become parents ourselves if we weren't at some level compensating for the problems, mistakes and vices we had first identified in our own parents.

Another source of teenage sorrow is how many big questions suddenly fill one's mind, not least: *what is the point of it all?* This questioning is also vital. The sort of questions that adolescents raise tend to get a bad name, but that is more to do with how they answer them than with the questions themselves. What is the meaning of life? Why is there suffering? Why does capitalism not reward people more fairly? Adolescents are natural philosophers. The true endpoint of adolescence is not that one stops asking huge questions and gets on with the day to day. It's that one acquires the resources and intelligence to build an entire life around the big questions that first obsessed one at 17.

Lastly, and most poignantly, teenagers tend to hate themselves. They hate the way they look, how they speak, the way they come across. It feels like the opposite of being loved, but in fact, these isolated, self-hating moments are the start of love. These feelings are what will, one day, be at the bedrock of the ecstasy these teenagers will feel in the presence of a rare partner who can accept and desire them back. Intimacy will mean nothing to them unless they have first spent many nights alone crying themselves to sleep.

Nature appears to have arranged things so that we can't get to certain insights without suffering. The real distinction is between suffering with a purpose and suffering in vain. For all the horrors of adolescence, one of its glories is that the suffering it inflicts is largely rooted in some of the most crucial developments and realisations of adulthood. These fascinatingly miserable few years should be celebrated for offering us a taste of the most fruitful kinds of grief.

19. Lessons in Limitations

In a painting by the 18th-century Swiss artist Angelica Kauffman, we are in the portico of an aristocratic home in Ancient Rome in the 2nd century BCE. A dignified widow called Cornelia has received a visit from a friend, who is enthusiastically taking her through some of the

Angelica Kauffmann, *Cornelia, Mother of the Gracchi, Pointing to Her Children as Her Treasures*, c. 1785

contents of a jewellery box on her lap. She's holding up a fancy gold necklace, she has expensive earrings and there's an encrusted belt around her waist. But Cornelia, though wealthy, has no interest in such things. Her dress is plain and unadorned; her hair is done up with a simple wrap. Her real concerns lie elsewhere: with her left hand, she is holding on to her daughter, Sempronia; with her right, she is pointing to her two boys, Gaius and Tiberius. And she is telling her friend lines that would have been known to all classically educated people in Europe from the Renaissance to the late 19th century: *'Haec ornamenta mea sunt'* ('These are my jewels').

In other words, people who truly understand the meaning of life know that it is all about children. Like Cornelia's, their attention is devoted to the welfare and education of the next generation. Their own satisfaction comes far below, as was demonstrated by another well-known scene from Cornelia's life embedded in European consciousness and repeatedly depicted by artists. When Ptolemy, the King of Egypt, tried to seduce Cornelia, and bent down to offer her the crown of his nation, the plain-living Roman woman was reputed to have simply pointed to her children and politely said: *'Nihil'* ('Nothing'). What was the point of love and Egypt when you could stay at home with the little ones?

Laurent de La Hyre, *Cornelia rejects the crown of the Ptolemies*, 1646

The story of Cornelia may have been repeated in art over long periods of history, but it was never considered normal. It was to parenting what the feats of Hercules were to physical prowess: an achievement to gaze up at, not a peak on which to expect to settle oneself. What marks out our own age is that the anomaly has become the norm. We are all supposed to be Cornelias now. Having and raising children with complete devotion is held up as a supreme but also a universal goal. It isn't merely one thing we might do among others; it is what we are all meant to do in order to lend our lives value. We may be drawn to alternatives – fame, money, travel, creativity – but none of these can truly matter next to what should be the lodestar of our concerns: our little ornamenta – perhaps now throwing earth at one another in the garden or (if the jewels are a bit bigger) lying in their bedrooms in the mid-afternoon, weeping or morosely texting their friends.

Despite Cornelia's impressive behaviour, and despite moments of extraordinary joy (those times when we gaze at them sleeping angelically in their goldfish-patterned pyjamas or receive them in our arms as they run towards us after a day at primary school), we probably have to admit to some darker thoughts that pass through our consciousness on a fairly regular basis. When we watch them arguing ungratefully with us, when we witness another of their tantrums over nothing, when we contemplate their careless habits, when we consider our scratched and rubbish-strewn homes, we may wonder whether Cornelia really had it right. We have loved them so much, we have sacrificed such important parts of our lives, but has it been worth it for anyone involved?

Sometimes, at moments of crisis, we are liable to face up to a few complex and taboo emotions. If we're honest, we may sense that we don't like our ornamenta much; we may even wish that they could go away and (in the nicest way possible) never have been born. We may feel that our love for them has not been enough. Far from redeeming our lives, they may have ruined them. We realise that we have given birth to humans, not angels. Some of the melancholy and bitter 3 a.m. truths run like this:

The role is impossible

We have been given an entirely unmanageable task, at which we were bound to fail according to the prevailing definitions of success. The children won't be exceptional. They aren't exemplary and we have made an untold number of mistakes, despite our passionate wish to avoid them. In the past, we might have got away with it. There was no such thing as a worry about being a 'good' parent. The only one who worried was the child; they worried about being good enough for us, about meeting our expectations and not letting us down. They lay in bed at night praying that they might become more decent people whom we would take notice of and like. Our role was so simple: it was to punish the child, point out their many failings in an unvarnished style, force them to follow our rules, insist that they marry the person we thought might be right for them (and us) – and then, if they'd been very good and nursed us in old age, we would leave them something in our will.

But as the world has become modern, the rules have changed. The parent is now expected to serve the child; we are meant to worry about letting *them* down. Any unhappiness in the child has become the fault of the parent; their failure isn't their problem but ours. Anything that goes wrong with a person, even a middle-aged one, can have only one cause: inadequate parenting in the early years. Parenting has changed from being a practical, domestic, discipline-based task to being a multifaceted feat that even a god would hesitate to take on or know how to handle.

Work and family
Unfortunately, the new ambitious ideals of parenting have developed at exactly the same moment as has modern capitalism. In other words, just as unprecedented demands have been made on us in our working lives, so too the parenting sphere has become more exacting than it has ever been. We are no longer expected just to show up at work in order to get a

wage. Work has thrust itself forward as the intended obsession of all admirable people. We are to come to work early and stay up late. We are to take up all possibilities for labouring on weekends and travelling to remote corners to attend conferences and congresses. We are to expend every last bit of energy in reaching the top of the corporate pyramid – this at exactly the point when society has also started to expect us to be home every night to read bedtime stories and to take an intimate interest in every detail of a child's inner life. Capitalism and childcare are at loggerheads, but neither admits as much; indeed, both sides torture us by promising that we might be able to achieve 'work–life balance', an ideal as sentimental and humiliating as expecting that someone manage to be simultaneously both a professional ballerina and a brain surgeon.

You are a punchbag

Our kindness towards our children, far from breeding respect and gratitude, has left us as the supreme figures of blame for every upset and reversal. Imagine that the blades of your child's remote-controlled helicopter have snapped after five minutes, just as you were starting to get the hang of flying it. The fault lies squarely with the manufacturers. But, sadly, they are not present in the kitchen – so, at once and not for the first time, you become the target for the raging disappointment of a 5-year-old. The repeated bad behaviour is surprising. You certainly weren't so tricky with your parents when you were young, but then again, you never felt so loved. All those assurances – 'I will always be on your side' – have paid off perfectly: they have encouraged your child to direct their frustration and disappointment onto the loving adult who has most enthusiastically signalled that they could, and would, take it. Your kindness has made you a punchbag.

You have to be the spoilsport

You wanted to be merely kind. In fact, it turns out you also have to be called a despot. Human nature has a strong bias towards whatever is most immediately pleasant and fun. And yet the central, unavoidable task of being a loving parent is to encourage the child to delay gratification in the interests of their own longer-term fulfilment. That's why there will be fights and they will be ugly. After all, it is much nicer to play video games than to learn how to spell 'scythe' or 'embarrassment'; it's much more amusing to see what happens if you paint your nails than to do maths homework; much better to read a comic than to brush one's teeth; much more gratifying to stay in bed than to have a career.

Out of love, a parent must be the representative of duty. And for this, they will be punished and slandered. They will be treated as if they had arbitrarily made up the mechanics of tooth decay and had themselves designed an economic system where the playing of computer games was disconnected from a capacity to pay bills. They will be punished for always bringing up unwelcome facts; for keeping reality in mind. And they will be unfavourably compared with people who give the child whatever they want, because they just don't care about them. It's the thoughtless hedonistic characters, the ones who suggest all-night cartoon sessions and come around with ice cream, who will be viewed as the heroes, while the caring, denying parent has to contend with being called a 'meanie' and, later on, and with particular vehemence, a fascist.

You have to exert authority rather than teach

At the outset, the dream is to coax the child into doing certain difficult things without having to demand they do so by force. The dream is never to have to 'exert authority', by which one means bypass reason in order to impose a conclusion. The dream is to teach and never to rely on the more basic weapons, like the reminder that one is the older, richer, bigger party. We want to meet intransigence with logic and calm. We want the child to do willingly what they had at first resisted passionately. One thinks with distaste of the Victorian parent demanding obedience simply by saying: 'Because I am your mother' or 'Because I am your father.'

To the child, the meaning of these words, 'mother' and 'father', has changed entirely; they now mean merely 'someone who will make it nice for me' and 'someone I will agree with if I see the point of what they're saying'. But attempts to appeal to a child's reason can only go so far. Whatever one says in a gentle voice, the child won't eat vegetables; they won't want to get out of bed in the morning; they will want to mock their younger brother or sister; they won't stop playing the game. When the child is very small, it is easy enough to deal with these protests: one can just lift them up or distract them in some kindly way for a moment. But later, by 6, one has to use authority: one sometimes just has to assert that one knows best, without explaining one's reasons.

The child can't have the relevant bits of experience that would render one's lessons comprehensible. A 9-year-old girl cannot understand how humiliating her 6-year-old brother physically is a bad idea because this might make it hard for him to relate easily to women when he is older. It isn't her fault she can't understand.

It would be unreasonable to expect a 9-year-old to correctly comprehend the force and direction of adult concern. The dream is that one will be able to pass on insights to the child that were painfully accumulated through experience, and thereby save them time. But in the absence of experience, insight doesn't work. One cannot rush children to conclusions; one cannot spare them time. They will need to make many of the same mistakes (and a few new ones too) and waste a good part of their lives finding out what we already know.

You can't make things too nice for them

Modern culture is vexed and appalled by the thought that development might require suffering. We have been traumatised by the barbaric, old-fashioned enthusiasm for punishment; the view expressed by generations of sadistic schoolmasters that success demands pain; that there is a necessary relationship between early discomfort and humiliation and later strength and 'character'. We have not merely rejected the old mechanisms for inflicting suffering (the cold showers, the beatings); we have for the most part sought to abolish suffering altogether. Kindness has been triumphant. Yet this attempt to abolish suffering involves waging a counterproductive and ultimately cruel war with the facts of human nature.

We know from our own experience that we have grown through things that had a painful side to them: that there were terrors, rejections and disappointments that made us more mature and better able to pursue our goals. We know that the drive to accomplish certain things, to master some difficult material, to win out over others gained some of its power from fear and insecurity. Because someone (perhaps a parent) didn't always believe in us, we redoubled our efforts. Because we were afraid of the consequences of failure, because succeeding was the only way to impress someone we loved who wasn't easily impressed, we put on an extra spurt. We desperately want our child to become mature, but without going through awful things. We hate being an agent of fear. We want always to cheer and to hug. We want everything to be nice. Yet we also know, in our hearts, that pain is an unavoidable feature on the path to a successful life.

You can't guarantee their goodness

The Romantic view of existence sees all humans as fundamentally good from birth: it is only upbringing and a lack of love that corrupts and damages us and, in the process, makes us cruel. Romanticism states that if a child can grow up anxiety-free, secure and encased in love, it will never break another child's toy, rip up their paintings or try to scare them. If a child has reliably been shown kindness, she or he will be reliably kind. But experience suggests the existence of some darker sides hardwired in us and beyond the reach of the gentlest behaviour; certain kinds of aggression, cruelty and wanton violence appear to be innate.

A child may just want to hit its sibling out of excess vitality, boredom or native sadism. It might just be fun to smack someone in the face to see what happens. That's why there used to be such an emphasis on manners. Those who upheld them didn't believe that a child could be spontaneously good simply because they'd been shown love. Indeed, a firm denial of love was necessary to help the child create a wall between what they might feel inside and what they knew they were allowed to express with others. Being strict wasn't a route to making anyone evil; it was a way to teach a person to keep their evil firmly locked up inside themselves.

You can't guarantee their success

The modern parent believes that it might be possible to mould a happy, fulfilled, successful human. From this flows the minute attention to detail, from the purchase of the cot to the timetabling of after-school activities.

It is this that explains the Mandarin lessons, the French horn, the educational trips to the countryside and the ruinous tutor fees – because with all this in place, fate and failure can surely be kept at bay. Yet the relationship between effort and return is more bizarre and more random. We cannot spare those we love the cup of human sorrow – whatever the intensity of our after-school programmes.

You will be forgotten

You take great care not to be frightening. You make silly jokes, put on funny voices, pretend to be a bear or a camel – all so as not to intimidate, so as to be approachable, the way one's own parents were not. It should be a recipe for reciprocated love. But weirdly, we rather like difficult people in a way we often don't nice ones – people we can't quite read, who aren't around so often, who are a bit scary have an appeal all of their own. They hook us in, in a way the kind, stable ones never do. One loses authority by being natural, approachable, friendly, a bit daft; the clown who doesn't want to scare. An even more dispiriting thought comes to mind. Love them reliably and without fear and you will be forgotten. Be distant, intermittent, often absent and deeply volatile, and they will be obsessed with you for life.

The life you are preparing
them for is full of pain

You are putting in so much work because, at some level, you hope that they can be happy in this world. But the facts of life are bitter; no one gets through it without agony. Watching them sleeping, you might want to tell them the following dark things: 'Darling, you'll have to do so much you don't want to do to get through this painful life. One day, many years from now, it will be 3 p.m. on a Tuesday afternoon and it'll be lovely outside, but you'll be analysing trends in electricity pricing in Belgium or chasing up a client who is deciding if they want to invest in a multistorey car park in Croydon (where you've never yet been). It won't interest you in the least, but you'll have to do it – because you'll have bills to pay and a career to uphold. You think homework will end when you finish school, but here's the unbearable truth we adults can't bring ourselves to tell you: having to do things you don't want to do goes on throughout your life. It is – in many ways – what life is. When you are in a relationship, you'll need to do things your partner wants, even though they have no appeal for you. You'll have to visit their awful family. You'll need to think of interesting things to say about a film you didn't enjoy. You'll have to make breezy conversation with their aunt, who rather frightens you, and with their brother, whom you find entirely dull.

'The agony will go on across a range of areas. Certain people will judge you in ways that are manifestly unfair – and you won't be able to do anything about it. Enemies will hate you for no reason. If you complain, you will be called thin-skinned; if you don't complain, they'll take your silence as an admission of guilt. You'll keep on thinking for a while that you can escape – that there will come a time when the suffering and incompleteness will come to an end. Perhaps after university, or after you make some money, or once you're married, or after you get divorced, or once the children have left home. You'll dream of a place and time without anxiety, suffering and feelings of loss and alarm. But you will never get there.

'All the while, you'll need to keep making enormous efforts and the fun times will get ever fewer and further between. You'll have to watch what you eat, even when you're longing to have another bite of carrot cake. You'll find that the most delicious things are fattening and that, at points in your life, you'll crave food as the only pleasure that you're allowed. In your leisure time, you'll have to make yourself do stretching exercises because your limbs will start to stiffen. One day, you'll notice yourself slowly but perceptibly ageing. Your skin will stiffen. Small lines will appear around your eyes. The bad photo of you from ten years back will exceed this year's most flattering shot. There'll come a time when you'll have to force yourself to make an appointment to see the radiologist; you'll have to accept the dreadful verdict, though it will obviously be insanely idiotic that your life, your dazzling inner existence, your sheer loveliness and beauty and your delight in seeing the sky and the trees will all come to an end in this senseless, strange, amazing and exhilarating world.

'Your life will in certain ways be a long sequence of different kinds of homework. Horribly, maths or French is the easiest version: a beginner's guide, almost a pleasure.'

They will damage your relationship

The hope was that your love for a child would deepen your relationship with its coparent, but almost certainly the opposite has happened. There is so much more to argue about and so many new areas for resentment. Two visions of child-rearing clash from the start over the cot. What does the crying mean? What is the best time to wake them up? Should they have banana or avocado? Each party will be trying to repeat certain good things from their past while avoiding the bad ones and, predictably, they will happen to be different things. One person will be in flight from an overbearing authoritarian manner; the other will be recommending boundaries and a decisive sense of command after suffering from the excesses of liberalism.

You will find yourself in passionate arguments over unknowable questions; it will never be entirely clear whether they need to be burped or walked around, study chemistry or take up geography, go on the school trip or stay home. What will be evident is that you will never have cared for an issue so much in your entire life and you'll be ready to have a loud argument to defend your line. Along the way, sex is likely to be destroyed. It seems so contrary to the atmosphere of a home with children. It isn't just practically difficult, it is conceptually awkward; physical intimacy and the love of children do not mix. How could someone who one minute was taken up with reading a bedtime story to a tender 3-year-old, suddenly shift to being in the mood to be tied up and flogged? As the Roman exemplary figure Cornelia implied to the King of Egypt, parental love can be the enemy of sexual pleasure.

Some of the problems are those of society

We live in a relentlessly apolitical age that attributes all mental malfunctioning to problems of psychology rather than those of wider society. There is only one explanation for children who can't cope: their family of origin. We don't allow that difficulties forming relationships or finding purpose, loneliness or anxiety might be the result of choices made at a macro rather than a micro level. Unfairly, we have personalised politics and ended up placing parents, and their presumed inadequacies, at the centre of the blame.

You will bequeath them new problems

By straining every sinew, we will have a good chance of sparing them our specific problems. We might have been scared of our parents, but our children won't have to be scared of us. We lacked material goods, but they will have plenty. But in seeking to avoid one problem, we are always at risk of generating another. Perhaps their lack of fear of us will lead them to an undisciplined and lax approach to their work. Or their material comfort will inspire ingratitude and lethargy. There are so many fresh ways for lives to go wrong that in sparing our children certain forms of misery, we are only heightening their risk of exposure to others.

Good enough

Despite all the difficulties, perhaps it is not a problem-free process we should ever really be after. The mid-20th-century English psychoanalyst Donald Winnicott, who specialised in working with parents and children, was disturbed by how often he encountered in his consulting rooms parents who were deeply disappointed with themselves. They felt they were failing as parents and hated themselves as a result. They were ashamed of their occasional rows, their bursts of short temper, their times of boredom around their own child and their many mistakes. They were haunted by a range of anxious questions: are we too strict, too lenient, too protective, not protective enough? What struck Winnicott, however, was that these people were almost always not bad parents. They were loving, often very kind, interested in their children and tried hard to meet their needs and to understand their problems as best they could. As parents, they were – as Winnicott put it – 'good enough'.

Winnicott pinpointed a crucial issue. We often torment ourselves because we have a demanding and impossible vision of what we're supposed to be like across a range of areas of our lives. This vision does not emerge from a careful study of what actual people are like. It's a fantasy, a punitive perfectionism, drawn from the cultural ether. When it comes to parenting, we imagine a fantasy of parents who are always calm, always perfectly wise, always there when their child needs them; whose offspring always willingly eat nourishing meals, play happily and don't want to spend all their time online. There are no parents and children like this. But a Romantic conception of the perfect parent can fill our minds and make us anxious and fretful, because our own family life looks so messy and muddled by comparison. Astonishingly and unreasonably inflated expectations leave us only able to perceive where we have fallen short.

With the phrase 'good enough', Winnicott was initiating a hugely important project. He wanted to move us away from idealisation. Ideals may sound nice, but they bring a terrible problem with them: they can make us despair of the merely quite good things we already do and have. 'Good enough' is a cure for the sickness of idealisation.

It is important to be merely good enough parents. Perfect parents would create particular headaches for children; they would set a standard besides which they would always feel like failures. Flawed but kind parents do their children an enormous service: they prepare them for the world as it is. With love, goodwill and plenty of mistakes, they ready them for the only life they are ever likely to lead: one that is deeply imperfect *but good enough*.

Picture credits